DEAR YVETTE

Shattered Fairytales

Dear Karla,

Thank you for supporting this best-selling Self-Love & Self-Acceptance movement!

Sending you our LOVE as you create Joy on your own life's Journey.

In Gratitude,
Yolanda Yvette Neals
aka
Mhogani Pearl

DEAR YVETTE

Shattered Fairytales

Liberating. Raw. Truth.

Plug into your power. Share your stories. Heal yourself and the world.

MhoganiPearl

MhoganiPearl Press • Atlanta

MhoganiPearl Publishing LLC
P.O. Box 450826
Atlanta, GA 31145

ISBN: 978-1-68026-011-3

First Press/MhoganiPearl Publishing LLC trade paperback edition February 2015

Cover artwork by Atlanta Brand Central
Book design by Maori Karmael Holmes

Manufactured in the United States of America

For information regarding special discounts for bulk purchases, please contact The RED Panty Society at 1-404-981-2367 or theredpantysociety@yahoo.com

www.DearYvettebook.com

www.theredpantysociety.org

Table of Contents

Foreword

by Doris A. Derby, Ph.D., Executive Producer

Dear Yvette is a personal story and a guidebook for life's journey. It is a great read for persons of all walks of life. It is for women and men, old and young adults, the married and the single, the professional, the non-professional, and the student who wants to find solutions to healing the traumatic experiences in their lives so they can move forward.

The book is a personal story yet it reflects the lives of many people. It is also a handbook for those who want to remake a path dissimilar to the one they traveled in their earlier life. It will be extremely useful for those persons who feel that they are mired in hurtful and harmful relationships, and want out of them but don't know how to do so. It is for those who desire tools to free, forgive and accept themselves, want to find love in themselves and others, as well as have compassion and forgiveness always in their lives.

Looking through the kaleidoscope of Yvette's life, MhoganiPearl depicts the intense and tumultuous journey of her shattered childhood and early adulthood with the intertwining of the original, and later developing, hip hop music and more specifically, the song, "Dear Yvette". While being physically, sexually and emotionally abused, exploited and abandoned, she suffered unimaginable things yet she survived with the same determination as her African ancestry did, with inner strength, and resiliency, combined with the necessity of maturity and responsibility for survival and a better life for her and her family. Yvette knew that she was promised this, deserved and imagined it was so, through the fairy tales she read as a child.

Through the vehicle of personal, one on one conversations the reader sees Yvette bloom into a mature, beautiful, self-confident woman exuding self-acceptance, self-love, self-forgiveness and compassion, as she learns to surround herself with poetic and spiritual affirmations. Lessons are learned through a revelation of Yvette's experiences, divine love and the power that is vested in her own hands, her mind, body and spirit.

Step by step, chapter by chapter, one sees life's stumbling blocks turned right side up, the challenges demystified, and a complete intersection of mind, body and spirit in her work, family and play with the actions, reactions and optional pathways which are available for successful travel and continuous healing.

Dr. Doris A. Derby is an educator, documentary photographer, author and Civil Rights activist. Originally from New York City, she served as the Founding Director of the Office of African American Student Services and Programs at Georgia State University in Atlanta, from 1990 to 2012. She retired after 22 years of dedicated and legendary service. Her documentary photos have been seen locally, regionally and nationally in galleries, museums, books and films. She is married to actor Bob Banks and they live in Atlanta, GA.

Thank You's

This book is dedicated to the billions of women and men who have been compromised and their greatness deferred due to unjust violations to their body, mind and spirit. These beautiful souls who bring forth awareness that make the world stop and command compassion. The humans who have been trafficked; children who have been molested; students that have been raped on college campuses and the soldiers being violated in the line of duty.

I thank my awesome, amazing, unconditional loving mother for being such a shining example of divine redemption. Mom, through your 27 years of remaining clean and sober, you have taught me to truly trust and believe in GOD as we overcome obstacles that are created for us and by us. Thank you momma for showing me how to grow into my greatness, in spite of my own life's hardships and mistakes via your own growth. You are truly are my SHERO!

I thank my sister and brother for being such awesome overcomers and showing up in your greatness despite all that we've all been through. I thank my beYOUtiful, wonderful, fabYOUlous children for allowing me to love them, care for them, direct and guide them the best way I know how. And for being such great reflections of how much I love them, unconditionally.

I love and thank the rest of my family and friends for your support on this amazing journey that I call my life! I thank my best friend, mentor, and beacon of what greatness is, Dr. Doris A. Derby, your friendship has blessed me infinitely. You are truly an angelic Agent of Change and I am grateful to have you in my life.

And lastly, thank you to my other best friend, Tien Sydnor-Campbell, whose shoulders I've been leaning on for EVERYTHING over these past 30 years! Thank you for being my mid-wife and helping me to finally birth this story. I Love You! Thank you to the other awesome sisters who also joined and supported my vision to give birth to this story; Monique Anderson, Brittney Sanders, Michele Madison and our earth angel editor, Kim Brundidge.

And thank you to the readers, for embracing this social movement for Self-Love and Self-Acceptance which is powered by Forgiveness and Compassion!

About Dear Yvette

Five African American women have come together as first time writers to collaborate under the pseudonym **MhoganiPearl** to tell the true-life account of a young woman who was once mentally and emotionally paralyzed by a childhood trauma. Two of these women are the main characters of the book, Yvette and Angela. The book chronicles Yvette's journey to find self-love and acceptance and is told through Yvette's therapy sessions with Angela, a certified body-centered psychotherapist. Through holistic affirmations, empowering letters to self, some Reiki and radical forgiveness work, Yvette manifests the perfect love—for her Self.

The foundation of this story is a woman healing negative beliefs associated with a turbulent upbringing, which includes her introduction to the old hip-hop song Dear Yvette and how it seems to mirror her situation and help shatter her belief in her own level of self-worthiness. Etched like a scratch on a record in her mind, Yvette began to internally, secretly hate herself after she heard that song. The song has an obviously misogynistic tone and stands out because of her name and the fact that most of the hip-hop music that she loved to listen to on the radio back then before that song came out was about uplifting, empowering and having fun, not tearing down or degrading women.

This story is based on Yvette's 40 year journey. Much like the trajectory of hip hop music, it is at times a drama, and at others a comedy, with meteoric highs and devastating lows. This is not a tale of sorrow or dismay, although at times it may appear so. The beauty of this journey is that Yvette not only survived but thrived and has come out of her experiences as a shining manifestation of true love.

As we circle the wagon in observance of the first 40 years of hip hop, it's time to have a compassionate, open and honest conversation about the language and images that have become synonymous with what's happening in the urban community. Let's consider how we've talked to one another, about each other, and how we describe ourselves via this culture. Especially in the midst of communities that are often already afflicted with so many traumas, let's have a conversation about self-reflection and self-healing. The time is now to come together as a global community, not to censor or indict the expression of creative freedom but to become more mindful and socially accountable as a village for the undeniable collateral damage that continues to undermine our community in exchange for material gain.

Note from Yvette

Pull up the song. Press play. Then close your eyes in almost a meditative fashion. Listen to every word you hear in the lyrics. Now imagine, that you are 14 years old and about to enter high school. You have been raped, molested, bullied, neglected, abandoned, rejected and you don't have anybody supporting you through these tough times because you suffer in silence which is also shadowed by shame.

What affect would this type of music have on you if you heard it over and over again, every time you sought to entertain yourself via music, television, videos, or parties to help ease your pain?

As the eldest child of teenage parents, I had to grow up fast. Before I knew it, I was helping to change diapers, going next door to borrow flour and sugar, taking mama's food stamps to the store to buy bread and cereal, and paying bills or making payment arrangements. I was forging my mama's signature by age 10 and having regular sex with my uncle by age 11.

Life for me was definitely not a crystal stair but I learned how to survive in the jungle! I mastered the mode of survival and as a young adult--hustling and surviving is what I knew best. But I learned how to do it intelligently, using proper diction and with a little class, so I fooled the masses. Most of the time I hid behind a mask, a mask that hid the pain connected to my desire to not just survive but thrive like other people who seemed to be living a much better life than mine.

A woman is never just a hoe or a slut. And a man is never just a thug or a gangster. There is always something deeper going on underneath than what appears on the surface. So it's time that we take a more intimate, compassionate look at what's really going on! (In-2-Me-I-See)

I am sharing my story with you with the intention that you will one day find the raw, real, relevant courage to share your stories with me too, so that all of humanity will be blessed with the many experiences that helped us all liberate ourselves as we create joy on our journeys back to Love!

In gratitude,
Yvette

Prologue

From Angela, the Therapist:

In fairy tales a child is born to two people who are in love with each other and the child. Parents are expected to not only take care of the most fundamental needs like food and shelter but also to encourage and uplift the child's spirit. They have a responsibility to create a physically, emotionally, and spiritually healthy person.

There is a widespread presumption that our mindsets, personalities, and behaviors--primary determinants of what we call *fate*--are set by the age of seven. Do you believe this is true? What if who we are is dictated not by the events leading up to the lighting of candles on our seventh birthday cake, but by the circumstances of our conception and birth? Or, more provocatively, by a culmination of the conception, birth, and context of the life events of our parents and fore parents?

Our experiences are housed within us and when unsettling events are left unsettled, they manifest as unrest in our attitudes and behaviors. Many seek to remedy the unrest singularly: spiritually, physically or emotionally, unaware of the connectedness. However, it is only through the undeniable connectedness of the mind, body and spirit that peace can be made with the self.

As Yvette shares her journey in the following chapters, take mental note of the interconnectivity of the self. Note how the body acts and reacts based on the mind's processing of events, actions, and subsequent reactions.

From beginning to end, nothing in our lives happens haphazardly. At the time of our conception, it has been divinely decided what needs we will be called forth to heal, and who will support us in that healing. It matters not how it looks or feels; everything and everyone we experience on our journey has a purpose and that purpose is to usher and direct our healing.

Even your parents were chosen by you because they fit the perfect prescription. Parents leave a lasting impression on their children's lives. From the time of conception up until the point the child begins to think for his or herself as an adult, parents are usually the biggest influence.

Before you can think for yourself you have to untangle from all of the ropes, strings, and chains that your parents may have inadvertently tethered to you. While bearing in mind that parents don't get handbooks and most do only the things that they know how to do: they mimic what they witnessed.

So who do you become when your father refers to your mother as a whore or a bitch?

Who do you become when the words spoken about the mother is playing on a loop in the mind of the child, and then the opinion is mirrored by what you hear on the radio?

Dear Yvette.

It doesn't matter how it looks or feels. Everything and everyone we experience on our journey has a purpose and that purpose is to usher and direct our healing. There is no one way to reach your truth. But understanding that you deserve to know, being willing to forgive and then letting it go will allow you to move closer to your divine purpose.

Chapter 1

Once upon a time there was deception...

Yvette enters the waiting area where she observes a sign above a basket that reads *Take what you need.* It contains tear-offs with the following words neatly typed on each strip: *love, peace, understanding, forgiveness, compassion, hope, patience, courage, and freedom.* On the table is another sign; this one reads *If you were waiting for a sign, here it is.* Yvette smiles.

There are paintings grouped above a line of comfortable chairs. On another table sits a tea kettle, an assortment of teas, packaged sweeteners, cream, and a bowl of sweet smelling, fresh fruits. Lulled by the classical music coming from the overhead speakers, Yvette relaxes and focuses her gaze on the warm blue adjacent wall where she is drawn to an interesting piece of artwork that looks to her like an expression of pain and release.

The therapist steps out into the waiting area. She is model tall, slim, blonde and beautiful.

"Yvette?" She says, extending her hand, "I'm Angela." And, with a firm, warm handshake she directs Yvette to the session room.

The session room's decor has the same warm feel and color scheme as the waiting area. There are pale blue and earth-toned walls, a plush sofa, more comfortable chairs, and a stuffed bear with a name tag that reads *Today.* The bookshelf filling the entire south-facing wall holds an assortment of books related to health, wellness, inspiration and alternative healing. Oddly, there's also an exercise ball, a treadmill, a stationary bike, and water bottles. The space is much larger than most. Each area looks like it could've been its own office--large but comfortable, full yet surprisingly uncluttered.

"So, Yvette..." Angela says, with an endearing smile, "Welcome. Allow me to tell you a bit about myself and what I do here. The methodology I use is a self-

love and acceptance approach. My professional background for the past 20 some-odd years is as a body-centered psychotherapist, certified massage therapist and Reiki Master. I specialize in helping others recognize that the body and mind cannot be separated, neither in health, nor in care. My goal is to help empower others in managing problems of the *bodymind*.

Through the sessions, our conversations will center on your life story by way of 5 year increments starting from conception to the present in an attempt to determine what's been deposited in your bodymind, impart counseling to expose the psychological material, and use the appropriate bodywork to process that psychological material. Some of the types of bodywork available for our therapeutic exploration are craniosacral balancing and Reiki, which are energetic healing modalities. I will use aspects of some or all of the methods that I've mentioned to help you reach your optimal level of recovery and self-empowerment.

The treadmill, bike and exercise ball aren't necessarily there for fitness--like you'd see them used in the gym-- but rather, they are there because it's sometimes easier to talk while the body is in motion. That makeshift booth in the corner over there behind the partition has a microphone and stool in it just in case you feel like expressing yourself creatively. My whole health methodology approaches the recovery and empowerment process with the understanding that a stomach ache is not just a stomach ache and a headache is not just a headache. How does this all sound to you, Yvette?"

"It sounds good to me. I'm ready", replied Yvette.

"Great! Then please have a seat and let's start at the beginning."

It seems like all problems start the same. They might end differently, but the origins are always the same-- deception. My life is no different. I started out as a secret. No one knew about me except my father and, of course, my mother Karen. She didn't dare tell her physically abusive father, Sonny, and she couldn't tell her strict, old-fashioned grandmother, Minnie. Her mother wasn't around, so that wasn't an issue.

So, from the beginning, I was a secret, because otherwise I would be living proof of Karen's disobedience: why else would she get pregnant? No one in her family could conceive of the possibility that Karen-- the problem-child, the black sheep-- might simply want a child to love on and who would love her in return. Who would believe that? Who would believe her? No one. So, from the beginning, out of fear, she hid me.

Why was she a black sheep? Because she was a self-professed disobedient child. She would leave the house and double back after her dad and grandmother left for work and she would have sex, drink and just hang out. My dad, Aaron, would smoke weed during these excursions --that was his thing. Mom was simply rebellious and determined to have her way.

Even my mom's decision at age 12 to move up north to live with her surly grandmother and her womanizing father was really about rebellion. My mom chose to live in the midst of abuse rather than stay in Florida with her mother Jessie and deal with no longer being the center of attention after Jessie had a new baby. Up north, my mom learned to withstand abuse because that's what her father modeled. Abuse was not only on the table, it was the centerpiece. Abuse set her standard for normalcy and by the time she was fifteen, my mom did "whatever" to be accepted.

For the first few months of her pregnancy, my mom Karen and the supporting cast of family members played their parts perfectly. If there were rumors about my coming, they were kept to a whisper. If anyone really knew about me, they didn't say a word.

For the first four to five months of my life in the womb, I was literally swimming in fear, manipulation and deceit. My mother was in an unsafe and unhealthy environment, attempting to conceal any physical evidence of my imminent arrival. In fact, she'd gone as far as to put iodine on a feminine napkin to sidestep Minnie's suspicions. "Poor child, is this the best you can do?" Minnie had said, fussing as she shook the pad she pulled out of the bathroom trash. Minnie was displeased, but she *did at least* take Karen to get prenatal care soon after.

My grandmother Jessie had three children back to back by my abusive grandfather, Sonny. When she finally got away from Sonny, she left my infant mother in South Georgia to be raised there by family until she could get back on her feet down in Miami. That turned out to take six years. I think because of that maternal disconnect, when Karen got pregnant with me at age fifteen, life continued as she knew it, disconnected. She continued having unprotected sex. She continued to drink. She continued to place herself and me, her unborn baby, in unhealthy environments and unsafe situations because she was so disconnected.

Do you ever watch those crazy talk shows about paternity? I feel like I see beautiful little beings, like me, being denied, rejected, overlooked, and abused everyday on TV -- not privately, but publicly. They show the children in close up on the screen. The kids are usually well behaved and quiet. People said I was sweet and quiet when I was a baby, too, just like the kids being broadcast worldwide for our viewing pleasure.

But you see how these shows focus on the main characters on stage - the parents? Mothers and fathers, for lack of better words, acting out, throwing temper tantrums in front of the whole damn world! Not one person considering how their behavior affects their child. When we watch these shows, we're watching real life playing out like a damn scripted reality show. You can hardly hear anything being said because of all the fighting and fussing. Oh, but I hear that fighting leads to great lovemaking so maybe that's what keeps these crazy cycles going.

Anyways, after the host calms everyone down, it usually starts again. The back and forth accusations and rumors are spit: "I didn't sleep with no one but you." "You a lying Bitch." "She a hoe!" "Man she fucks everybody." "He a hoe, he ain't shit!" "Fuck you bitch!" Eventually the young lady starts crying and screaming, "I don't want yo' triflin' ass to be my baby daddy anyway." All the while we know she really does. We know she wants to be validated. All this he-say-she-say bullshit isn't hard to fathom. Just imagine a life filled with chaos and lies; decisions and judgments based on rumors. How ridiculous is that, right?

Well, it was in this kind of vicious cycle that I began my life's journey. One that was unstable and volatile from the get-go. A breeding ground for self-doubt, self-hate, insecurity and a host of other self-defeating and deprecating issues. And just like the people on TV, my parents have different accounts of what happened, who did what, and how or when they did it.

When my mom retells it, she says she was just a kid having a kid and didn't know what she was doing. Just like *her* mother Jessie, Karen ended up having two more children back to back by the time she was eighteen! The magnitude of being a parent didn't even occur to her until years after she was already three people's momma!

And if you ask my dad, all was well. They were a picture-perfect family and he just wanted to be a good provider. Yeah right, let him tell it! But there's a scratch in his record too. Just like my grandfather, there were rumors of my dad being unfaithful and abusive, and it didn't stop, even after my young parents married and continued to create the rest of our family. There were more babies, more drama, more fighting and more drinking and eventually drugs.

> **Yvette, your conception and birth narrative illustrates how your mother's experiences may have affected your development. Her experiences are also your experiences. We will spend more time talking about this part of your life so that both you and I have a better understanding of the things that make you who you are today. Allow me to point out a few things I think are significant regarding what you've shared up to this point.**

Were you aware that the mind has the complex ability to suppress or discard things that may be too hurtful to recall? The significance of this is that you shared your mother's feelings of being fearful, undervalued and deceptive from the very beginning of your life in utero. I don't want you to feel that what I've said is an indictment of your young parents. I want you to have an understanding of the impact of your experiences in utero.

There aren't any scientific studies that say 'this equals that'. But it's common for health practitioners to promote a stress-free environment for both the health of the mother and the growing child. Through clinical experience, I can attest that many mothers who experience mental and emotional difficulties in their external environments, when asked specific questions about the mental and emotional climate of the internal environment during pregnancy, have recalled the presence of fighting, generalized unrest, and anxiety about the future.

They verbalized similar experiences of fear due to inconvenient pregnancies, as well as social and emotional issues with the children's fathers. These issues resonate with many women and I want you to know, Yvette, you're not alone."

Oh, I understand that now 40 years later. Although I didn't realize when I was growing up, that other people had jacked up families too. Like for instance, according to my mother and father, the main issue surrounding my birth was that I was born with jaundice. There's no doubt in my mind that Mom understood this to be nothing more than a condition common in newborns. Clearly, she didn't understand that this was validation of the energy that I literally marinated in for 9 months. Can you believe that? I read in a book that jaundice is the mental and emotional result of conflict, a chaotic pregnancy. The fact that I was born to young, black, teenaged unwed parents -- I guess the stereotypical prejudices that come with that was a breeding ground for conflict and chaos!

Anyway, the jaundice kept me in the hospital for three additional days. I guess, at the time everyone thought that's all it'd take for me to get better, but if I understand the book that I read correctly, the damage was already done, and far more of it than any one could've known. My mom took me home like anyone else would have. Again, not understanding the gravity of it all, I knew mothers passed a lot onto their unborn children, but not *everything*. Pregnancy is already enough of an emotional roller coaster in and of itself--add stress, judgment, anxiety, and fear of the possibility that all of these things could be passed to your baby-just like eye color. That is really something else!

Yvette, you're right. Jaundice is very common and its treatment reflects current thinking that it's related to nothing more than a hiccup in the infant's adjustment to life outside of the womb, something to be taken care of with special lights. But it doesn't just happen to every baby.

While even a mentally and emotionally healthy pregnancy can result in a baby born with problems, what's important to our conversation is the fact that the birthing process can be a very stressful event, one that even in modern medicine still sometimes needs intervention and treatment. Looking through the lens of stress and anxiety that pregnancy can bring, it's not a far reach to see the impact of mental and emotional issues birthed on the newborn.

Your jaundice could easily be associated with the increased emotional and mental stresses that your young mother endured during her pregnancy. However, since it isn't an ongoing mental or physical issue, let's move further along and consider other factors. Tell me about your early childhood memories."

Well, my mom eventually landed a great job... well, great for an 18 year old anyway. Back in the day, working a factory job in the Midwest was the shit and for the first time in her life, my mother was making what they called 'good money'. This job made her the breadwinner; she was supporting our family. This also meant that the bulk of her time was spent away from us, and we were left in the care of our loving and devoted babysitter, Tanya.

My mom routinely worked long hours, so it was normal for all of us to be asleep by the time she came in. She told me that one day she came home early and me, my brother and sister were all in our beds asleep. Well apparently so was Tanya—she was asleep, intimately spooning right next to our father, in our parents' bed!

Not knowing what to do when she saw them, Mom walked out of their bedroom and closed the door behind her. She poured herself a drink and sat down on the couch in the front room and cried. To say she was hurt would be an understatement. Just when she had started to make something of herself, this shit happened. While she was out working hard to provide for her family and her husband, this bullshit is going down, in her house and right in her own damn bed! After a couple of drinks, my mom woke them both up and all hell broke loose!

My dad recalls this event as a simple misunderstanding and maintains he was never unfaithful to my mother... You know what I know now? That unhealthy, broken people hurt other people with rumors, lies and deceptive actions. I definitely displayed the effects of this young chaotic crazy love from my parents throughout my life, whether I knew it at the time or not.

What I hear you saying, Yvette, is that you recall a feeling of mistrust starting very early. Up to 18 months, if you aren't able to trust others, it shows up as distrust of the self. Emotionally, that's attached to poor self-esteem, self-confidence and self-respect. Since we're not going to separate the mind from the body I want to know if you've had problems with digestion and or mid to lower back pain.

Yvette answers "yes... yes I have. It's not constant but it definitely is worse when I am stressed about something."

Yvette, this is not your standard villain-to-victim

pathology which is common in fairytales, but rather one of victim-to-victim. Yvette, you are a victim of victims. Your parents could not possibly give to you that which they never received from their parents. As much as they may undoubtedly have wanted to, and as hard as they probably tried, there is no way that they could give what they neither knew, received, nor were in rightful possession to give. Instead, what they give are the broken pieces of themselves in hopes of somehow making you whole.

As common, and undoubtedly true as this is, it doesn't discount the high probability there still exists a wounded, young Yvette inside of you. A girl who doesn't fully know who she is because her parents didn't fully understand who *they* were. A girl who feels abandoned. A girl created to fill a hope for, and longing to belong. A young girl who was once encased in a womb of fear, shame, and deceit.

Although you can't change the conditions of the past, you can begin to heal the wounds by uncovering your truth. To accomplish this, you must first begin by being there for yourself. You must show up for the little girl within you, because she needs you.

"How do you show up for yourself?" Yvette asks.

Believe it or not, the adult version of yourself has what it takes to comfort your inner-child. Showing up for your inner-child means first being emotionally honest, expressing how and what you feel with truth and integrity.

Showing up means acknowledging the fullness of your feelings. Showing up is offering support; letting your inner-child know she is loved, no matter what. Let her know that she is accepted, no matter what. If your inner-child is feeling abandoned, hurt, ashamed, and even angry, know these are just the many ways she's been conditioned to say, "I am afraid." These words are all code for fear.

Abandonment says, "Because my needs were not met in childhood, I am afraid I do not have what it takes to meet my needs as an adult. I am afraid to be emotionally honest for fear that the love and support I need will be withheld from me." Hurt says, "I am afraid of the big scary world out there. My own environment was unsafe and unstable, and these wounds are mine, they are a familiar hurt and I am afraid to give them up for fear of greater unknown hurts."

Shame says, "I felt neglected, invalidated and unimportant. I am afraid to show up as myself. I am afraid to be rejected." Anger says, "I feel resentment for the things I didn't receive as a child, but I am afraid to seek a new way of expressing my hurt." Anger says "I am afraid of being hurt, so I use anger to create a safety barrier around me, driving others off in fear."

The good news of all is that you are all grown up now. You have the tools and the means for physical, emotional and spiritual self-sufficiency and fulfillment. You are free! You are free to be exactly who you are. And, you are perfect just as you are. So today, you can begin to make better choices for yourself and your inner-child. You can choose love over fear. You can love yourself enough to admit that your inner-child is wounded and afraid of abandonment, full of hurt, shame, and anger. You can allow your younger self to feel the full range and extent of her emotions. Assure her that her feelings are perfectly hers, perfectly fine and, she is perfectly loved and supported on her journey. Show her that it is not only vital, but fully acceptable and, even encouraged that she shows up as her authentic self.

You must show her that, although her journey's

beginning was full of lies, confusion, shame, and fear, she can and must consistently make the choice to stand in her absolute truth. And, in that truth, she will face down her deepest fears, in the darkest hours with full recognition that she can still move forward in love. Angela smiles.

"Wow Angela! That is deep. And it feels so true for me." Yvette says. "It's beautiful how you made the beginning of my life make so much sense. I've never been told the truth in a way that feels like that before."

"Well, you've come to the right place to learn and explore your own truth for yourself. I want to congratulate you on having the courage to seek and process your truth in a way that will allow you to grow and become what you truly desire to be in your life. This is just the beginning of several sessions, so I thank you for being so open and willing to share your story this first time.

Just so you know, my version of therapy includes homework, so that there is a combination of physical action as well as mental and emotional work to help move things through both the psyche and the soma, which are fancy words for the mind and the body. What I'll have you to do first is read this letter to your 1 to 3-year-old self. Angela reaches for a manila folder just across her desk and presents Yvette with the following 3 handouts:

Dear Young _____,

I know that you are afraid. I know that you've experienced feelings of abandonment, hurt, and even anger about your circumstances. It is well within your right to be afraid. It is perfectly fine for you to feel disappointment, ashamed, and confused, considering what you have experienced. I am here for you. I am here to love, comfort and protect you. I accept you just as you are. You are an esteemed part of me; we are one. We come together in perfect formation of the whole. We no longer have to live in the past. We no longer have to live with the hurts of the past. We can choose to release this hurt that causes us to fear the future, together today. From this moment on, we can choose to show up as love. Let us allow the richness of this love to spill over creating experiences of peace and joy.

In love,

_____

AFFIRMATIONS

I am always safe and supported.

I freely give and receive love.

I am loveable.

Even when I am afraid, I can still move forward in love.

I love and accept myself just as I am.

I love, nurture, support, and protect the little girl in me.

I am who and how I am and I matter.

When our parents are not in tune with who they are, they will undoubtedly fall short on providing us with what we need to discover who we truly are. A mother can't give to her child what she doesn't have.

If we could each paint a picture of our perfect story, it would surely begin in love, support, and nurturance. We'd choose to be born of parents who have it all figured out. Parents who are sure of themselves and their role in our lives. Parents who know that every thought, every word spoken, every deed done or left undone will affect the child, and the child's emerging portrait of his or her self.

However the truth is, in real life you don't get to erase the picture if it doesn't come out as envisioned in your mind's eye. What you get is a call for acceptance of your picture, no matter how ugly or frightful it is. Your parents are not picture-perfect. Your story is not a fairy tale. It is real life.

In real life, children give birth to children who sometimes grow into wounded adults, attempting --amidst much struggle and adversity-- to take on the roles abandoned by their parents when neither parent is aptly attuned in a sense of self to raise, support, nurture, and love the child in the way he or she needs to be loved to ensure complete health.

Such individuals don't understand what it means to provide a loving environment. They're not equipped to give what it takes to be emotionally supportive. Unsure of how to truly love themselves, they are most assuredly unsure of how to completely love anyone else. And, here the cycle is perpetuated: a wounded adult-child--a child who has birthed another child--will undoubtedly pass on the hurt, fear, abandonment, shame, and rejection cycled from their original wounds. Hurt people do hurt people.

What I'll have you to do is please read over all three of the handouts and then begin reciting the affirmations daily. In our next session together, I'd like for you to begin by reporting any significant changes you feel in your body and mind as a result. "Remember", Angela says slowly and emphatically, "the body and mind are undeniably connected."

Lastly, after you read through the handouts I've given you, I'd like for you to answer a couple of questions for yourself. We can discuss them in the next session if you'd like, but they are designed namely to assist in your own personal growth.

Ask yourself, are you more critical of yourself than others? And, do you feel both trusted and trustworthy?

Angela gently touches Yvette's shoulder as they both head towards the waiting area.

Chapter 2

Come on, ease on down, ease on down the road
Don't you carry nothing that might be a load
Come on, ease on down, ease on down, down the road
— Ease on Down the Road (The Wiz) Charles E.
Smalls

These were relatively good times. School was easy for me because I was a natural student. I was reading at age four and totally in love with learning by age five. I was very bright academically. I truly enjoyed the welcoming acceptance of my teachers and I was just about every teacher's pet. But this is also the time in my life when the shit really hit the fan. A lot of stuff happened...a lot of really fucked up stuff.

After all the drama, my momma had to let the fairytale go, white picket fence and all, because fairy tales don't leave folks hanging. In fairy tales folks don't work 12-hour days in a factory to provide for their children and then have fucked up endings like ya' momma and daddy fighting all the damn time. Once upon a time never ends with ya momma being thrown out of her own house butt naked and locked outside literally for hours, by her own husband. In fairy tales, the princess doesn't have to witness this type of crazy ass un-fairytale type of bullshit between her momma and daddy over and over again.

Eventually, my momma left my daddy's ass, never to return to him again. If he had been the only problem, maybe we would have lived happily ever after, but he wasn't. Instead, my momma was now a single mother of 3 making it work the best way she knew how. My dad was in and out of jail for all different types of reasons, so he wasn't around to be of much support. So my mom turned to my daddy's family and her father for help during these years. In return I got closer to my daddy's mother, Grandma Carolyn, and my momma's father, Grandpa Sonny.

I loved me some Grandma Carolyn and Grandpa Sonny and all that came with them! I was such a happy, precious little girl.

Joy seemed to ooze from me. I naturally knew my role and the leader that I was to become. I was the oldest of the three and a natural born leader. I was extremely helpful with my siblings. It was organic to me. I was special and everybody recognized it. I naturally followed my spirit unquestioned, even as a child.

I was in heaven when I went to school! I would jump out of the car every morning running and waving back, like bye momma! I loved school and I fit right in! The teachers loved me. There, too, I was a natural helper.

By this time, my mom was stable and more focused on being a good mother. Well as good as she could be to her children while still working twelve-hour shifts six days a week. My love for school was obvious, because I wasn't the type you had to make do my best, I always wanted to do my best! Since I was so great in school, my mom took on another job so that she could give me the best education. By the time I was in fourth grade, she enrolled me into a predominantly white private Christian school. Good stuff, right? Not!

Classism and racism were still an everyday part of life for most of America in the late 70's and of course I wasn't excluded. The neighborhood, at that time, was not really all that desegregated. And that second job my mom took was at the private school I was attending. The problem was that she was the cleaning lady in the cafeteria at a school full of entitled little snotty-nosed ass white kids! It was here that I learned to turn the other cheek, but I promise you I don't see how Dr. Martin Luther King Jr. did it!

While I did get a "great education" at this school, I also got a "great education" on life at the same damn time; an education that fed the fear, insecurity, judgment and pain that already existed in my life. Before I was ten years old, I learned how to live with great disappointment on the inside while smiling on the outside. There's no one on the planet who could deal with this type of torment -- constantly being attacked for being too black around the white kids and too white around the blacks. I was called everything from aggressive to Oreo, and I suppose turning the other cheek just helped me fall in line.

I didn't bully anyone like I was bullied. But I bullied myself by
trying to imitate someone else's life. It was definitely during
this age range that I became inauthentic. I moved away from
my organic self just to survive. I was forced to change in order
to avoid so much teasing, taunting and disrespect, so the cycle
of people-pleasing began here. Who wants to have to physically
fight every day to defend who you naturally are? Not me. I am
naturally not a fighter. But by imitating others, I eventually had
to fight.

Sometimes physically, sometimes verbally but at all times I was
fighting. Fighting inside against my own heart. Tears may not
have flowed on the outside but they ran like a river on the inside
because I couldn't believe that people were so damn mean. Little
by little, I began to shut down. Trapping my truest feelings inside
as if they didn't exist. More pain and more confusion continued
but I somehow knew to never let them bitch asses see me sweat.
So I shined at school, a girl from the hood reaching for the stars
and rising to the top.

Then things changed. One day, my mom took us to see a movie
called "The Wiz". The one starring Michael Jackson and Dianna
Ross. I was blown away! Inspired and in awe of what I witnessed
on that big screen, my life changed forever. I fell in love with
music from then on. Even though the ups and downs of my life
were still in full effect. I had music now, as a way of dealing with
the neighborhood drama and the drama of school. Music allowed
me to keep 'easing on down the road, just like the characters in
"The Wiz".

Because my mom worked so many hours, my siblings and I began
spending many hours with our grandpa Sonny. Grandpa Sonny
got me my first job at the restaurant his friend owned. I started
out sweeping the parking lot and making 4 dollars an hour. Soon
I worked my way up to cashier. I was comfortable with being in
charge and now I was right where I wanted to be in the midst of
all the business. Grandpa Sonny had two "step daughters" that
he was raising with his white girlfriend, Tina. I was cool with
both of the girls but exceptionally close to oldest daughter named
Trice. Trice and I had kind of a co-dependent relationship. Trice
was this cute blonde-haired, blue -eyed white chick who wanted

to be in with the black crowd and I wanted to get credit with the white people at school so we formed a perfect relationship. She was my white "auntie"!

By this time my mom had a *third* job driving a preschool Head Start bus. That woman would work her butt off to provide for us, but that shit was out of balance. Because my mom was at work most of the time, the opportunity for us to do whatever we wanted, whenever we wanted to was ripe for making what I now realize were wayward decisions. My ten year old self was spending all of my free time at the local hangout spot on Samson Street. This is the street that my Grandpa Sonny lived on, a popular street where kids hung out to do God knows what, all in the name of unsupervised fun because all of our parents were off working all of the damn time!

I was getting older and more curious by the day so boys were always on my mind. Not like they were when I was six, because they were just friends then, but by age ten, they were potential 'boyfriends'. Samson Street had all the goings on and a bunch of boys my age that were ripe for the liking. There were several sets of boys to choose from: the Packson family had at least 7 potential playmates. The Pike boys, the Jenkins boys and the Elliott brothers were all available to give me the attention I needed.

I liked playing with these boys and one boy in particular, Jason. I knew exactly what I liked about him. His green eyes and slim, light-skinned build. The street football games they used to play quickly turned into other type of games, the touchy feely type of games that lead to other thangs. I liked Jason a lot and the other boys liked me. Well at least that's the way it seemed. I loved the attention the boys gave me. I liked being liked, even if Jason in particular didn't like me. So I did things to be liked, even if it wasn't the right thing to do. I was living an unsupervised existence and making choices that an unsupervised ten year old little girl was bound to make.

Hide and Go-Get It became the game of choice. I got real good at hiding where I could be found by the right boy -- Jason. There was a whole lot of chasing and getting caught. There was some feeling touching and kissing. There was some of that infamous dry humping going on, too. These were the good times! My siblings and I were having lots of fun daily, especially in the summer months during this period.

Being popular meant people liked me and I wanted to be liked so I continued to frequent Samson Street as much and often as I could. My Aunt Trice, my teenage co-conspirator, was my guide. She was almost twice my age, so mimicking her may have made me a little too grown!

All the access to the popular boys and a growing sense of insecurity was changing my sweet little life in ways that I could not yet begin to understand. At this point, I was a normal sexually curious preteen, one might say. Others might say something not so nice, like I was hot or fast but there were no concerned adults around most of the time to say *anything*. They were always working, so we were often finding our own way.

> **Yvette, let me understand what you've shared and shed some light on what it sounds like became a way of life from this time. You attended a school that didn't help you feel comfortable in your skin. Your *brown* skin. This can't be dismissed too quickly. There is no doubt that the impact of being teased for being a child of color in a predominantly white school meant that you didn't feel this to be a safe space or place.**
>
> **Know this: our ability to remain sound in our innate sense of self sometimes falls prey to the environment we live in. At this age, freedom of self-expression is natural. It is natural to need to know that we are safe to be ourselves. You don't have to be perfect. We need to know that even so-called mistakes do not define us or reflect our true self-worth. During this time, Yvette, would you say you felt the support of anyone?**

Oh, yes. Then? Then, my mom was very supportive and active with me and my siblings. I'm telling you, she was a mom in a supposed real kind of way. Then... it seemed like she was getting the hang of what it was all about. I was a Brownie via Girl Scouts.

I was in dance school, playing the trumpet and singing in the choir. After my parents divorced, we went from a house of chaos to one of comfort. We were now, finally, living in a loving and nurturing atmosphere. More and more, things were looking up.

My mom had me, my brother, and my little sister dancing and singing wherever she could showcase us. And, there she was, beaming with pride like any other young mother, 'Look at my babies"...look at my toys. She still didn't get it though. Although I enjoyed the attention, and we were having fun...I wished it was *her* attention, I guess. But don't get me wrong. My momma worked her butt off to provide and take care of us. The good thing about Samson Street was that I could be my fun-loving self, unlike how I had to be at school. Even though I wanted male attention, I was living life authentically, or so I thought.

Listening to you talk about the events of the past, it's important to remind you of the way this looks to both your child-self and your adult-self. When we're not sure of who we are and how to fully stand in the authenticity of our true selves, we attempt to be" perfect". Authenticity is the exact opposite of perfection. Authenticity is knowing that you're not perfect, while still allowing yourself to be perfectly you. We're born with a curiosity and propensity to seek knowledge; humans love to learn. We enter this world with a strong sense of self; we know exactly who we were created to be. As children, we know what we like and what we don't like. We know what we want and what we don't want. We know what makes us happy and just the opposite. We know who we are and for the most part we're not afraid to share it. We give of ourselves freely. We say what we feel and how we feel. We express our emotions freely. We partake in things simply for enjoyment. As children, we are our most authentic selves.

I think you'd agree that what you've shared thus far speaks likely to your true character. This period in your life is when the psychological development of self-confidence happens for most youth. Thankfully,

you were exposed to additional support systems that met your needs, including your strong thirst for knowledge, at a time when learning how to fit in became important.

One of life's true blessings and privileges is the right to become who we truly and completely are, and not just the pretty pieces. Much like young Yvette, many of us trade in that right, our most authentic selves, for a secondary version that helps us survive the trauma of childhood.

This is the only way to adapt to such an oft-traumatic environment. We become who we think we need to be in order to receive what we think we need to survive.

No other species is charged with the responsibility of evolving and living simultaneously. Human beings, innate curiosity seekers, must learn to create a balance in life that makes authenticity and the fearless pursuit of self-knowledge their ultimate goal. Our main objective is to become astute in the knowledge of self and fluent in its acceptance. We must be unwavering in the understanding that all of our experiences are divinely designed to move us toward the prize.

So Yvette, we are going to be moving into the next period in our next session, but before we do, do you feel we have fully explored and addressed the most impactful experiences of this time period?"

Yvette nods confidently as she gathers her purse and belongings.

"Good. Before we close today's session, let me give you some new questions to think about, another handout, an empowerment activity, and some more affirmations I'd like you to recite before we meet again. I'd like you to ask yourself, what are some of the things you did in childhood that you still do as an adult? And, are you able to walk away from people, places, and things that are bad for you? I want you to think about this time period as you answer these questions and consider any and all mental and emotional stresses you faced during this phase, including thoughts of feeling safe and secure within your family, school and community settings; the feeling that you could stand up for yourself or the feeling of being at home wherever you were. And, lastly, any issues of following household and social rules -- were any or all of these strained during this time period? You don't have to answer these questions right now. I want you to really think about them before answering. OK?"

Angela smiles as she reaches for the letters and affirmations folder and hands the papers and her questions to Yvette.

When our innate need for learning is nurtured, we are given permission to be fearless and to make mistakes on the road to discovering our likes and, equally as important, our dislikes. The avoidance of mistakes is not a fool-proof recipe for success. Consequently, it can be the roux in a perfect recipe for disaster. Through our trials, we learn not only what makes us tick, but what drives us. We develop the tools essential in obtaining the right kinds of attention and acknowledgment needed to thrive.

If a child only gets attention from a parent for bad behavior, and good behavior is met with silence or indifference, then the bad behavior is likely to become the preferred standard of behavior for that child. Additionally, a child who has a tumultuous home environment filled with anger or violence may look to school as a haven; this can also be problematic. Typically, the school day is a succession of organized and orderly exercises and activities. Children in diligent pursuit of knowledge are the staff's primary focus. Conversely, naughty children are met with disdain, stern words and isolation; admonished and sent to the dean and principal's office.

So, how does one become fearless when they may not feel completely comfortable being their authentic self in an environment? Children have two primary settings: home and school. If the home setting negativity is pervasive enough to force a child to wear the armor of an adult, it can prompt the child to take on the onus of responsibilities neglected by the parents. And in the school setting, although the adults are performing according to regulated tasks, the child may feel the only way to survive is to become a model of perfection. This means mistakes are not an option.

At some point, we are all faced with the decision to focus

31

our energies away from things that maim us emotionally and spiritually and to direct them toward more positive, uplifting people and endeavors. We believe human beings have a built-in ability to switch gears if something or someone is not right. We believe self-preservation to be innate and autonomous. But, is it?

We are undoubtedly born fearless; our experiences however, create an internal environment that shapes us and keeps us bound. Is it possible to regain fearlessness and move toward authenticity and self-knowledge while navigating the emotional crawl-space that separates our polarized worlds?

Dear Young _____,

*It is okay to be who you are. You are Divine. I don't expect you
to be perfect and I accept you even when you make mistakes.
I don't expect you to be anything other than who you truly are
and I accept you as you are. You are the most true and organic
part of me. You are the _____ parts of me. I know that your
environments didn't offer you the _____ needed
to be true to who you are, but today I promise to fully love,
support and encourage you. I commit to being your safe haven.
You are safe with me.*

*You are safe within me. You matter to me. Your feelings, your
thoughts, your dreams and aspirations matter to me. I summon
you from hiding--show yourself! Show up however you choose. I
welcome you with open arms. I invite you to color outside of the
lines of life; release the need to be perfect.
Embrace authenticity.*

*I encourage you to remind me what it feels like to do things
solely for enjoyment. I want you to know that I will always be
of you as you will forever be within me. From this day forward,
let's show up together. Together, we are the expression of divine
authenticity.*

Yours truly,

_____,

AFFIRMATIONS

Each day I must show up as my true self, for myself, even if it means by myself.

I embrace my authentic self; it is a blessing and an honor.

I allow the truth of who I am to sustain me.

I was created to be authentically me.

Who I am is a gift to this world.

I am an individualized expression of The Divine.

I am my most authentic self.

I release the need to trade in myself for the approval of others.

Who I am is non-negotiable.

Chapter 3

... so the grey-beard stole twice or thrice round the house, and at last jumped on the roof, intending to wait until Red Riding Hood went home in the evening, and then to steal after her and devour her in the darkness.
*   – Red Riding Hood*

"Can I read something that I wrote in my journal to you" Yvette asks Angela as she enters the office.

"Sure", Angela replies. That would be a great way to start this session off."

"Actually, I'm a little nervous, so I think I'm going to read it from inside the booth over there" Yvette says as she walks over to the booth in the corner of the room.

(Reading from her journal)

I felt like a leaf swept up by the winds. Recklessly tumbling where the winds did take me. Going nowhere—like a treadmill. Travelling without moving, my entire existence was dependent upon the whims of the wind. Where it would stop, when it would stop, shit—can it or will it ever stop? Who knows? I was caught up, pushed, pulled, contorted by forces way beyond my control. Alone, like a leaf broken free from its branches,—no mommy, no daddy— no tree, no roots. I can remember thinking, calling out to them from the voice in my mind, 'Where the hell are you?' Screaming, 'Daddy! Where are you? I fucking need you!

Where the fuck are you? Don't y'all see me? Can't you see what the fuck I'm going through? I need help God damn it! Can I get a hand or a fucking break? Can I get some love? I need some love. Shit!' I mean, ain't that what every child needs? But no one heard me. My mother rarely, if ever, showed up and neither did my dad. So, left to my own devices, I learned to silence that need. Actually, I traded it in and filled the void where I could with whomever and whatever I could. I was just eleven then. Eleven. I'm out here now, off the chain, just doing all the wrong damn things for all the wrong damn reasons.

Unsupervised and wild, shit I was the supervision. I got my brother and sister right 'long beside me and they're right up in the mix."

Yvette concludes with the flip of her hand. Then she exits the booth and walks over and sits down on the plush couch.

"Wow, Yvette. That was pretty deep. Thank you for sharing that! Tell me, how are you feeling right now?" Angela asks.

"I actually feel a little relieved right now. I was kinda nervous before but I just jumped in the booth to read this and get it over with. So now I feel better because it's over with", Yvette laughs.

"This developmental period, Yvette, looks at the skills of demonstrating courage and independence or guilt. Based on what you have already begun to share, it sounds like you developed a self-starter attitude and, on some level, you felt disconcerted, particularly regarding your role as caretaker of your younger siblings. Feelings of guilt seem to be making an appearance in your day-to-day, and from that perspective, this would be considered a successful stage of development. What concerns me is what this mix of events will later reveal.

Let me also add, if any of this becomes too uncomfortable to sit through, the treadmill is an excellent place to work out some of the experiences that may be more difficult to articulate. Please do continue."

Around this time, momma got a new boyfriend named, Stanley. Stanley was a good guy; he made good money too, working for the Department of Transportation. He worked long hours just like my momma tho'. Stanley had four children of his own and due to their own drama—some abuse is what I heard—two of the kids had to move in with us. We had the room to spare, so I guess, why not. Our house, hands down, was the shit...we had the baddest house on the block. It was totally on some high class ghetto fabulous shit. Grandpa Sonny was a carpenter with skills and he cut a hole in the wall and put the TV in it, then built mirror doors to cover it so people wouldn't know it was a big o' television when we weren't watching it. This was way before flat screens and entertainment centers! We had an all-white room and an all red room. My momma had worked so hard to provide this palace for us to live in and my Grandpa Sonny hooked our shit up!

Anyway, here we are now five unsupervised children, three girls and two boys, ages seven through eleven, running around. Idle minds, idle time and that meant nothing but trouble most days. The new additions to the family only worsened the bad situation. School was still a mess, the neighborhood kids were a mess and now the mess could no longer stay outside my doorsteps. My younger brother and sister were in on it now, too. Everyone had some mean, negative, hurtful thing to say about me...except the boys.

Boys—11 and 12-year-old boys made me feel wanted, accepted and desired when it felt like everything else in my life was wrong, hurtful and unsafe.

> **Angela interrupts: In traditional psychology, this developmental period is concerned with identity of the self within the family, school and community structures, and how different roles are played out so that one can develop confidence. When this doesn't happen, confusion is created within the individual. What you've shared sounds like you were experiencing limited safety within those structures hence you began to armor yourself in different spaces. When you let your guard down it was because you felt like it was safe. Does that sound accurate to you?**

Yes. And there's more to the safety part of the story. My bad-ass uncle Alonzo, who is 3 years older than me, moved in with my family around that time, too. This was a disaster waiting to happen because he was a mess. My mother had the best intentions, moving her younger brother in with us. The goal was for him to help with the child care, keeping him busy enough to keep him out of trouble. But that was a fucking joke! Shit, his name should have been Trouble!

Alonzo was a delinquent. He didn't do better even when he knew better, it's like he just couldn't do better. Dark and shady, just like bad weather. With his presence, we now had a user and abuser in our midst. Alonzo was a thief, too. He would break into places and steal other people's things. He was always lying but too slick to get caught.

It wasn't long after Alonzo moved in that he joined us and the other neighborhood kids in the game of Hide-and-Go-Get-It. He was supposed to be there to look after us, but instead, he was right up in it with us. He came in and created even more chaos. Alonzo turned the small fires of mischief into a dangerous and roaring inferno. I remember like it was yesterday, my little brother Junior's 10th birthday party. It was a sleepover and Alonzo chaperoned because my mom couldn't stay...or just didn't stay. I don't know. Anyway, tell me why me and my sister ended up freakin' dry-humping every boy at the damn party? Ain't that some crazy shit?

Well, this was the type of thing that he was there to prevent from happening, only it is precisely the kind of thing that *did* happen under Uncle Alonzo's "supervision". It wasn't much longer after Alonzo's unwelcome arrival and my 11th birthday that the next untimely arrival happened – I got my period. And, as usual, my mother wasn't around. But Stanley was.

Stanley really was a great guy. I'll always remember him and how well he handled my period situation. I honestly didn't know too much about periods. My mom just didn't have that conversation with me. I knew very little about feminine hygiene as a whole. And, what I did know, I picked up from reading my Judy Blume books.

When my first period arrived—I'll never forget, it was on a

Saturday morning. I woke up, saw the blood, and just sorta... well, panicked! I changed my bloody panties, put some clean ones on, stuffed some tissues inside the clean ones, and went on with my usual Saturday morning routine — football out in the front of the house with the boys. Well, just as I was heading out to play and to throw the messed up panties in the trash outside, Stanley stopped me. For some reason—maybe the guilt of having my period...I don't know, I just felt caught, and I froze, freaked out, plopped down on the couch and stuffed the damn bloody panties between the couch cushions! I can't recall now what he'd actually stopped me for, but it was nothing, really. So, I just went out and played football. For a little while anyway, until Stanley called me back into the house. This time, it was something. He had found the panties!

Can you believe Stanley had placed the bloody panties in a plastic bag? I couldn't believe it. I was so embarrassed, but he handled me and my period gently and lovingly. He explained that it was perfectly normal and natural for a girl my age to start having periods and assured me that it was nothing to feel embarrassed or ashamed about. He wanted me to know how great getting my period was, and told me I was a young lady now. He hugged me and assured me that everything would be fine. Later on that day when my mom called on her work break, he relayed the news to her so that she could get the all the things I needed.

When my mom came home she completely freaked out. Completely. I actually had to calm her down. She came home with everything a young lady needed. Stanley and I were close, and I truly loved him.

Thinking about this now, I'm really grateful for what he did for me that day. I was a young lady now and, truth be told— even with as good as Stanley had been to me— I still felt most comforted by my momma's presence.

Life didn't stop because I had my period though. In fact, after the brief freak-out and the short-lived love- fest with my mom, everything was everything again. Except for my relationship with Alonzo. He stopped treating me like he did everyone else. Yvette paused. "I think I wanna get on the treadmill now because I might need to walk this thing right here out." Yvette frowned as she walked over to the treadmill and began walking on it slowly.

Alonzo was a master manipulator and we'd soon find out that he was a predator as well. He had big plans, oh yes he did. All of us kids were left under his supervision more and more and this would prove a bad idea - a really fucking bad idea. The stakes were high and Uncle Alonzo decided he was going in for the take. Me. He took from me the only thing I hadn't bartered for attention, for popularity, for anything. The one thing I hadn't given to anyone. The one thing I wasn't ready...I was not willing to give. I mean, I was just a kid...just a kid. But just like a fucking thief, Alonzo stole what was mine, and meant only to be *given*. First he invaded my home, later my room, then my bed...and now my body!

"Let me get off this thing before I get pissed off telling this story", Yvette says as she climbs down off of the treadmill and returns to her seat on the couch.

> **"You're fine", Angela said. "Just take a couple of deep breaths for me, through your nose, then hold it and release it out of your mouth with a sound. Yvette takes three deep breaths and continues with her story.**

I was in complete shock and immediately turned on my side where I would stay for the entire ordeal. I was so tense. I tensed up immediately in response to his presence in my bed. And the tension increased as he pushed and pushed his Vaselined penis against my body. He pulled at my clothes, and he put his fingers inside of me. There I lay, still, silent, on my side in increasing states of tension, horror, and disbelief.

I didn't utter a word. I didn't move an inch; frozen and bewildered by what was happening I couldn't muster a response, an action, a thought. I knew only that this was not right. This—what was happening to me— was wrong. But, I couldn't bring myself to move or speak.

Thinking back now, maybe my stillness, my silence was a concerted effort to will it away, to will him away. I was thinking he would just stop. Maybe he'd stop after fingering me. Yeah, that'd be all. I was used to that, well, not like this. I liked it and wanted it when I played Hide-and-Go-Get-It with Jason. But, this was different. It wasn't like he was touching me in a way that I didn't like or anything like that...yet...I mean, I didn't know what was so different, but I did know. Y'know? I just knew this was not the same thing, and I did not like it. I did not want it!

Alonzo started to coach me along the way as he took my panties off. I couldn't for the life of me wrap my head around what was about to happen. I was stuck. I gave no resistance; I just let him take 'em off. I was a child. I was a virgin and Alonzo's penis looked enormous to me. I was afraid. He began to push and prod, forcing himself inside my tight vagina. Slathering on more and more Vaseline to ease his unwelcome entry. The more he pushed, the further I withdrew into myself, emotionally, physically, every muscle tensed. No movement, no sound, no words, no tears, nothing.

And he had to be numb— unforgivably, thoughtlessly, unscrupulously, Vaselined dick in hand, heartlessly numb as he stole my virginity, just thrusting in and out of me until he got off. Sick motherfucker! Is this what you do to a child? I was a fucking little girl!!!! Yvette cried out with intensity.

He took from me like I was his; entitled, beholden to him, like my pussy was his pussy, his possession. I was his *niece*! I was eleven fucking years old. And, I never gave him permission! When he was finished, he left my bed, my room— he left me right there, still laying on my side, withdrawn and bewildered. And, he left, as if nothing had happened. He molested me and left me to deal with the hellish aftermath. Who could I tell? How would I tell? Where could I turn? I was sad, defeated, deflated, embarrassed, ashamed and—alone.

And even that wasn't enough. Alonzo was so fucked up that he had the nerve to use his knowledge of all the prior games we played as leverage against me. The games were all a set-up. He introduced games so twisted that he went as far as to coerce

43

my younger brother and I to dry hump on each other. And, he watched so that he could later hold it over our heads...mostly mine. I was completely powerless, leveraged between fear and shame. This is ingrained, most memorably as the beginning of the end of my self-esteem.

Chapter 4

Yo Yvette, there's a lot of rumors goin' around
They're so bad, baby you might have to skip town
See something's smellin' fishy and they say it's you
All I know is that you made it with the whole damn
crew
— *Dear Yvette, LL Cool J*

I was an eleven year old hostage of fear, manipulation and perversion. Alonzo threatened to tell about the games if I ever told on him. Although, I know now that the offenses are in no way comparable, I didn't know that then, and in turn, I didn't know what to do. I was so afraid and confused. I had unwittingly entered into a pact with Alonzo. We had a deep, dark secret, he and I. One I'd keep bottled up for years, and as long as I kept it bottled, he'd keep it going. I died a little more inside as it went on, over and over and over again. At least twice a week, there he was, armed with a hard dick and Vaseline, and there I lay pretending to be asleep. Trapped. I was trapped by the world, by my home, by my family, and now, by the shame of this dark secret.

I yearned for freedom, normalcy, protection, I yearned for my dad. I missed him so much and longed to be fathered, loved, guided and protected by him but he was always somewhere else. He didn't show up for me, either. Although I did so all the time, I never got used to fending for myself. I knew -don't ask me how- but, I knew it wasn't supposed to be this way.

Angela pushes the box of tissues closer to Yvette and silently checks in with her. "I want to thank you, Yvette, for sharing something that I know is difficult for you to recount. It is clear from what you have shared today, that you continued to experience increased feelings of abandonment, and a general lack of safety in your home, community and, even school. One thing that's come to my attention is your physicality since you started to recount these harrowing events. Your physical development is very commanding. Using the psychology of the body tools,

I'm going to tell you what I see and you can tell me if it makes sense. OK?

I see what presents as character armor that you've built from this developmental phase. It is in your hips and thighs. Let me tell you why this is significant and you'll tell me if you agree. Your hips are a shield that armors and protects the self, the family and, the family unit. This is a part of the development of both the first and second chakras in energetic philosophies.

You know a little something about chakras, yes?"
Yvette nods her head yes as she wipes her nose with tissue. "Some other associations with the placement of this type of armor include pride and procreation. Do either of these resonate with you and how your body developed from this time period moving forward?"

Yes. After this began happening with Alonzo, my body started responding. I was having some issues- female issues, and it was definitely because of the sex we were having, or actually the sex he was having with me. So, you know I already told you I didn't know much about feminine hygiene at the start of my period. Well, apparently being sexually active meant that I should have been taking even better care of myself down there and, I didn't know that either. I was just doing shit. I was just growing into a little lady, y'know? Minus all the little ladylike shit. My lady parts were not right. At all. This was a problem, a big problem.

I started to notice a change in the way I smelled down there when I would use the restroom. My vagina now smelled... bad. Before the Alonzo thing started I smelled different-in fact, I didn't have a smell down there at all. And, now I did! And, it didn't smell good. And soon, it got even worse, as the smell was soon accompanied by a discharge; this liquid that was just...ugh, disgusting. Oh, it was the worst smell ever! I didn't have any clue what was wrong but I knew something was very wrong and, I couldn't tell my mom. I didn't know what it was exactly, but I knew well enough to know that it had everything to do with what was going on with me and that damn Alonzo. That much I did know. And, I wasn't telling my momma shit! I was not trying to get in trouble. So I just dealt with the smell and the discharge with more tissue in my panties. I figured, if it worked for my period that time, why not. Of course that didn't work out for very long.

It started to itch really badly and I knew it was just becoming a bigger problem as time went on. The itching was simply unbearable. And in a combination of ignorance and desperation, I got the bright idea to use Listerine to remedy this situation. The bottle said, Kills germs. So, I cleaned my vagina with Listerine; the outside and some parts of the inside, and it burned like a motherfucker. But, it worked. Well it worked enough to suit the mechanics of my twelve year old mind. The smell and itch went away, and thank you God because I don't know what I would have done if it hadn't. I used Listerine for the next two years of my life 'curing' whatever ailed my vagina, all the while continuing to have unsafe sex with Alonzo.

The argument for your bodily reaction to dealing regularly with so many shame incidents, including dry-humping your brother and enduring repeated sexual abuse tells me that the padding in your hips is a reminder of your body's need to protect itself against aggression. It looks like all of the conflict in this period indicates that the trauma affected the soma- remember that is the body- and, even if you appear to process and understand the psychological aspect of it as a life lesson, you suffered multiple violations from multiple events. If I were to ask you what you recall feeling in your body from the time of the first violation, could you tell me what it was like?

What I remember most is how I contracted my body and my vagina so tightly, probably to keep him from getting in...I don't know. I know I held myself quite stiff... and, still. I also remember that he always entered from behind me because I was either sleep or playing sleep.

Ok, Yvette, this is important. Do you still do that with current sex partners?

Oh my God. Yes. Yes, I do. It's actually something my partners have expressed enjoyment over when we're having sex-the tightness. I am also instantly turned off if a partner approaches me from behind without me inviting him to do so. I have gone off, you know, become angry and cursed them out because that still triggers me to this day!

I see. Knowing this now, Yvette, it is of utmost importance for you to come to terms with how much of a physical hold past events have on the body. Being abused at eleven years old by an uncle who penetrates you with his big greasy penis is neither forgettable to your mind or your body. While it may not have seemed violent, although it was violent, it is still a violation nonetheless. Do you understand that? Yvette nods in agreement.

From the first time the abuse occurred, Yvette, you must know that you did nothing to warrant it! You must also know that, as a child, there was no way for you to control or prevent that situation. Even if it doesn't feel like it has a hold over you today, your body remembers and wants to address it. When a child is eleven years old and is forced to submit to sexual abuse, the experience has to have a place to live in the body and you are holding that memory in your vagina. So take a moment to process what I have just said. Do you have any thoughts?

"No, not at all. Not right now, no." Yvette says, as she shakes her head at the same time. "It's all true. And, now that I am aware of why I do these things, perhaps I may come to enjoy sex more."

Have you not enjoyed your adult sex life? Angela asks.

"Not as much as I'd like to. I enjoy it, but I have a really hard time reaching orgasm. It's hard for me to totally relax enough to fully enjoy it. I make sure they-my partners-are happy and satisfied, but that's about it. Now, though, after hearing this, I kind of feel like I will go about things a little differently because I didn't consciously realize that I was basically reacting to being

48

molested."

"We can certainly spend more time on this area, but I'd like you to get back to where you were during this time period in your life because we aren't done. " Angela sits back in her chair and Yvette takes a deep breath and then continues.

At home things continued to decline. My best friend in the whole wide world has died without any real notice, my paternal grandmother, Carolyn. She had been my real escape from the madness at home. I never told her about the molestation because I feared that she would kill everybody involved, but I loved going to see her because I was always safe at her house. My mother lost her job at General Motors; which became the catalyst for her own personal decline. It would appear the idle time, idle mind adage applied to her as well. It took her no time to find trouble, and she found her trouble in the form of drugs. She and Stanley broke up and instead of searching for another job; she joined a motorcycle club and would go off with them for three and four week excursions at a time, leaving us anywhere and everywhere. It was crazy! We just abandoned our own house.

We (my brother, sister and I) ended up living with one of her friends who was an extreme ex-military guy. He had cameras and audio recorders wired all throughout his house, which allowed him to keep an extremely close and creepy watch over us. He was also very strict and obsessed with turning us into "obedient" kids so we got whipped for a little bit of everything! It took us about 3 months of constantly being whipped before we realized that a lot of what we were being whipped for was stuff that he heard us say behind his back as he spied on us via his home intercom system.

That became clear one day when I shared with my siblings that I was going to break us out of his house arrest by faking like I was going to school and instead going back to our house so I could see if our mom had finally made it back so that I could plead for us to come home.

I left for school that morning, intentionally didn't get on the school bus, and instead walked several blocks to our house only to see this maniac standing on our porch waiting for me. I got the worse whipping that I have ever experienced. Afterwards, he made me wear some old raggedy clothes that he'd purchased from Goodwill to school to teach me a lesson. A couple days later, I took a bath at his house, which *always* felt uncomfortable to me, and on this particular day, I was washing my body and glanced up to the window which was up above the bathtub only to see him looking down at me. I burst out crying. I remember feeling so defeated in that moment. I just wanted out of that place! And who knew what he would do next! So I made my mind up that I was leaving that place and this time I wasn't going to tell *nobody*!!!

Ironically, I had a bus token that one of my mom's friends gave me in case of an emergency before they dropped us off to this creep's house. So I decided to try missing the school bus one more time but this time catch the city bus to my dad's sister's house on the other side of town to see if we could come and live with her.

Monday morning came, I grabbed my coat and backpack and headed to the bus stop. Just my luck, the city bus came shortly after I got there. I jumped on that bus like a runaway slave heading north to freedom and didn't look back! I made it to the east side of town and got off near my aunt's street. Walking down her street, I encountered this large Great Dane dog that was loose in a yard about a block away from her house. I took off running for my dear life. By the time I reached my aunt's yard, I was screaming to the top of my lungs with the dog on my heels. My aunt came running to the door and at the same time the dog jumped on my back and pushed me down to the ground. I was so scared I peed all over myself.

Eventually, my aunt got me into the house and into clean clothes. After I told her the story, we drove to the drill sergeant's house but he wasn't there. I had a key so we packed up all of our belongings and left. Knowing that his house was rigged with recorders, my aunt talked shit the whole way through his house and dared him to contact her if he had a problem with it. She picked up my brother and sister from school and we lived with her and her 5 children for the remainder of the school year (about 6 months). All these changes granted me a reprieve from Alonzo and his sexual abuse as well.

Mom eventually came back from her cross country motor cycle escapade. She rented another house right across the railroad tracks. By this time, momma was really on drugs and partying a lot. The house was always full of motorcycle riding male friends of hers and they were often into having fun. We moved back in with mom, mom moved Alonzo back in with us, and he went right back to molesting me. Only things were different now because now I was bigger and, he and I fought...a lot!

I didn't fully understand why at the time, but we just did. It was also around this time that I realized I wasn't the only girl he was having sex with. I thanked God for that. I felt a sense of relief on some level, thinking he'd finally leave me alone, but that didn't happen. Alonzo was still Alonzo, manipulative, cunning, and predatory. The addition of more girls would come to mean only one thing, more drama. Now, I found myself arguing over petty shit with the other girls he was having sex with.

One girl, who had initially been one of my best friends, became my worst enemy when she and Alonzo began having sex. This bothered me- it bothered me a lot, actually. It just didn't make any sense. She was my friend, and to my knowledge, she didn't know that he was sleeping with me too, so I didn't understand why she was always so damn angry with me. But, I knew on some level it had to be Alonzo's doing. He had to be the blame for her issues with me because nothing else made sense. Nevertheless, it got to a point that every time-and I do mean every fucking time Pat saw me, she wanted to fight me. I hated fighting. I hated fighting with a passion, about as much passion as she had for fighting me. And so we fought, and fought again, senselessly, needlessly, endlessly; we fought that whole damn summer!

Back then, all of us teens and preteens used to frequent the community center parties. For twenty-five cents, all of the neighborhood kids could party on Fridays from eight until midnight. And, because Alonzo was Alonzo, there were often girls there who'd end up fighting over his instigating' ass. Alonzo was the older dude. The one many of the young girls were crazy about. Sometimes they'd even get the party shut down! Other times, they'd reserve the fighting for the parking lot after-party.

One Friday night, Alonzo was parading around the party with my ex-friend Pat. Well, that song 'Dear Yvette' came on. You know the song? Alonzo starts running around the party all crazy, rapping right along to the lyrics and egging' on the other guys to do the same; pointing out different girls like the song was about them! Then Alonzo got all up in my face with that mess too, but I pushed him away from me. And Pat had the nerve to get mad when I pushed him! Hell, I'm the one who felt disrespected! Every time the chorus came on all the guys would look over at me and sing it. "Dear Yvette. Dear Yvette".... Yvette mocked.

I didn't find that song or what he and the other guys were doing funny at all! I just wanted to leave. I was so upset, and I felt so insulted. Besides, the night was just about over. I started rounding up my girlfriends so we could all leave, and Pat started following me, walking behind me, teasing me, and talking junk by repeating the lyrics she'd just heard Alonzo and the others saying. I ignored her ass. I knew full well this fool just wanted to fight again. I had enough of fighting this damn girl. So without waiting for the others, I made my way towards the parking lot with just one of my girlfriends. But Pat continued to taunt and follow behind me, getting louder and louder. She was getting to me, too. I felt tense, and I was mad as hell, but all I kept thinking, was God please don't make me have to fight this damn girl again. I really hated fighting. But then, she shoved me from behind. Still, I held it all in, tense but composed, until she punched me-right in the side of my head! Hard!

That was the tipping point! Man, I turned around and beat the brakes off that damn girl. It was mostly a blur, but I could see glimpses of the others-her friends and mine were also fighting and arguing. Eventually, we were all surrounded by the other partygoers-onlookers. And, Alonzo.

Although he was at the center of all the bullshit in the first place, he and some of the other guys pulled us apart just as the police were arriving. The police began clearing out the crowd, and while that was all going on, I managed to get away from Alonzo, Pat, and the police, and into a friend's car. My friend got me home safely that night.

Word on the street was, I won the fight. But as soon as Alonzo got home, he would swear up and down that "his girl" won. I can't say I expected anything more from his simple, twisted ass because he wasn't shit.

Chapter 5

She knew this was the last evening she should ever see the prince, for whom she had forsaken her kindred and her home; she had given up her beautiful voice, and suffered unheard-of pain daily for him, while he knew nothing of it.
        -The Little Mermaid

Things just weren't the same anymore, and I wasn't the same girl anymore. I was fed up with having sex with my Uncle Alonzo so I began to resist him. That was a problem. And I couldn't, for the life of me, imagine why when he had plenty of other girls who actually *wanted* to have sex with him. Why wouldn't he just leave me alone?

So one night I really wasn't feeling him, and I told him to get the fuck out of my room, just as he entered armed and ready. By now I was just tired of it all. I didn't want him touching me! But, he just laughed and dismissed me. I finally threatened to tell on him! I was serious too. I didn't care, but he insisted. The more he insisted, the harder I resisted. I stood my ground that day. I feared it would become violent as he pinned me down, but I broke free and ran like hell, straight towards my momma's room. I was really doing it, I was really gonna tell on his punk ass! Fuck that, I was done and this shit was about to be over. I'd had enough! I was really gonna tell my momma on Alonzo for the first time ever!

But that amounted to nothing-nothing at fucking all. I ran towards my momma's room yelling for help: 'Mom tell Alonzo to get out of my room!' No response. None! 'Mom! Momma!' Nothing. When I reached her room I saw why. She was *high*-high as the fucking moon. Damn! As usual, she wasn't fucking there for me! I mean she was barely there physically but mentally her mind was gone! I had to deal with this shit by myself. Damn! What the fuck? God! 'You Bitch!' I screamed as I slammed my door and collapsed onto my bed, broken-just completely fucking crushed. 'When will you ever show the fuck up for me, momma? Damn it!' I cried out. I don't even know where his punk ass was while this was going on. I guess he ran off like a bitch when I started calling for my mom. But he would return-oh and when he did. He pinned my face down into the pillow and fucking took it! He took it like he didn't care nothin' about me at all. I was just some pussy. Yep, that's how I felt, like a piece of pussy. There was nothing about the experience that I desired, nothing that I wanted, or liked-nothing. Nothing at all. All I wanted, all I could think of was to wish he would leave me the fuck alone and just die!

I wished I could just disappear. I couldn't take it. I couldn't take this anymore. I was just broken. I broke down. I crumbled, I imploded, deteriorated into nothingness. I was... I don't know... I was just so hurt!

This transformed me. For the first time, I let tears flow; the tears that I'd held back for so long. I could no longer stand numb to what was happening-to what had been happening to me. In this moment, I felt the fullness of it all. I let myself feel.

I cried so hard that night, I mean I really cried. I was so hurt on so many levels, and I was helpless and alone. I cried because my mother wasn't there-still...again. I thought, I ran to you for help and you did nothing! You let him do this to me and you were fucking high! Stanley wouldn't have let this happen. I cried because my fucking daddy was somewhere else, not being a damn daddy to me! Not protecting me and keeping his little girl from harm! I felt all those things, but what should I have expected? What would my momma do, even if she wasn't high... what could she do? What has she ever done? I cried and I cried. I really wanted him to stop touching me. To never fucking touch me again. I wanted out!

He had treated me with such disrespect. No respect for me, and none for my body! I was too deeply wounded to hide it any longer. I felt taken advantage of, robbed-like something was taken from me. I felt violated and unimportant. And, I cried because I had no one. There was no one to protect me. I felt alone in the world. I felt raped!

This was the first and the very last time I would cry over sex with Alonzo, or in reference to Alonzo, period. He was a closed chapter in my life, as far as I was concerned. I would quietly turn over a new leaf. Mum's the word forever, I wasn't ever looking back.

Yvette holds her face in her hands and stares across the room in deep thought.

After several beats of silence. Angela finally says, "Looking at some of this in hindsight, Yvette, the trauma of not having your mom to protect you on this occasion could cause you to shut yourself off from engaging fully within relationships today. Would you say that this is accurate or not an issue?"

"Yeah, I can see that", Yvette tearfully responds. "Sometimes I get very upset and start yelling and screaming when I don't get what I want from people, especially when it's someone I feel I should be able to trust!"

"Do you think you reverted to survival mode to make it through each abusive event and the other violations? Do you also think that you may be doing the same thing now?" Angela asked.

Survival mode? Hmm... Yeah. The first thought that comes to mind right now is how I ended up using my long-time crush, Jason, to survive from getting exposed about Alonzo. I was 14 when he and I were dating during this time period. He had no idea what I'd been going through with Alonzo, no one did.

I could never lean on him or anyone else for support-not for that, I was too scared and embarrassed. I was really alone in this. But, I really liked Jason, and finally he liked me.

Jason spent a lot of time at my house; he would sometimes sleep over to hang out with my brother; that's how much my mom liked him. Jason truly was my escape. He was a distraction, but I also just really liked him. He didn't know I wasn't a virgin. He assumed I was and I just left it at that. My thinking was, he's good to me, so why ruin his fairy tale, you know? He had no clue, nor did he need one.

At some point, while Jason and I were dating, after Alonzo and I were done, I got the 'sleeping sickness'. I was sleeping all the damn time, groggy, dragging along and behaving completely out of character. My mom, during a sort of sober phase, asked me what I thought was a stupid fucking question at the time. 'Are you pregnant?' To which I replied, Uh...no!' All, duh-like, y'know, because honestly, I didn't think I was pregnant. I wasn't thinking about that shit at all. Could you just imagine how that would look? Who could I tell, what would they think? I just never let the thought cross my mind.

Well, did me and my mom argue about that shit! My mom just knew Jason had gotten me pregnant. And, it was just as well because the truth just was not an option. I was not gonna allow that to happen, and although Jason and I had never had sex-I wasn't in a rush-but with all of the sex I'd previously had with Alonzo, I had to have an alibi. I needed a scapegoat; I needed my momma to believe she was on the right track. As fucked up as it was, it was what I felt I had to do to survive; and so I did it. I intentionally, with a clear mind, had sex with Jason to cover the fact that I was having sex with my Uncle Alonzo, should this pregnancy thing be real. Somebody, anybody had to be the father of this baby, just not my Uncle Alonzo!

After a day at Planned Parenthood, sober or not, my momma was right about this one, because yep, I was pregnant! That much of it was true, even if she had the rest all wrong. I knew for a fact the baby was not Jason's; there was no way it could have been. Even still, I let...*led* my momma, her friend, and Jason—shit, I led the whole world on with this lie. I was pregnant by my mother's baby brother, my Uncle Alonzo and I couldn't bring myself to stomach that truth. I was sickened at the mere thought of it! Oh, but there's more...

Not only was I three months pregnant, I also learned that I'd been living with chlamydia-a fucking venereal disease! Feeling completely devoid of life, there was still even more to this drama. I was dealt the final blow...It had already been decided by the adults involved - my momma and her motorcycle-riding nurse friend who worked at Planned Parenthood, that I was having an abortion, and that's just what happened. I had an abortion at fifteen years old.

It was really a surreal experience. It was the worse pain I had ever felt. I just submitted to the process and was actually happy that I wasn't having a baby once I fully realized that fullness of my situation.

The gravity of things did come together in bits and pieces for me. I was beginning to understand life a little more. I learned that fucking without protection led to vaginal issues, venereal diseases, and pregnancy. I recall feeling overwhelmed, quite confused and I was slowly becoming more and more detached. I wanted badly to escape my reality. I needed a change, a life change, or at the very least, a living situation change.

Angela let the moment hang, then said: "What I appreciate hearing you articulate is that you were clearly able to know and understand the difference between what you chose to do with your body in having a sexual relationship with a boyfriend and, what it took to survive in your home environment, including sex with an uncle who demanded your silent cooperation for sex through coercion.

Just so you know, the development of sexual energy is a part of this time period, as well. Sexuality connects us to our own bodies and physical needs and, in this instance, for you, it was introduced through sexual harassment and abuse by your uncle. The chance you took to stop him was a very empowering moment, even though it didn't turn out as you'd expected. You have to know that your body mind was no longer willing to accept that situation, and the way you handled it was an awesome display of courage and strength!

Think about what it took to finally confront someone who had been controlling you with abuse, silence and secrecy for years. I feel empowered hearing your story. That shift may have improved your trajectory, but I won't know that until we get to more of the

story. Looking at the psycho-physiological impact of this time in your life, energetically, the emotional material descends into the lower abdomen and affects the bladder, pelvis and hip areas, including the sexual organs. What is interesting in your physical presence, Yvette, is that you have a very dominant pelvic region with a large buttocks and hip girth. These features are fairly common amongst us women of color, but did you know it is also very common to see the same mental, emotional, and physical issues as you? Especially amongst women of color, feeling powerless, victimized, and dealing with abuse, the physical issues known to stem from this phase include dysfunctions of the lower back and descending to the legs via the sciatic nerve. Other known issues include sexual potency, and obstetrical and gynecological imbalances.

It is common medical knowledge that we women of color statistically experience more obstetrical and gynecological dysfunction in comparison to women of other races in the United States, although there is no direct scientific rationale to account for the difference. As black women, we have higher rates of everything including infants with lower than average birth weights to increased percentages of sexually transmitted diseases up to and including HIV.

For the purpose of my work with you, it is only important that you are aware of these issues so that you may take precautions with your physical, mental and emotional state moving forward. An awareness of your own physical, emotional, and sexual boundaries is critical for all women. The ability to enjoy sexual relations and know when it is the appropriate time to engage in them is not always possible. Neither is knowing and understanding that vulnerability is not a shortcoming and that being violated and exploited has nothing to do with allowing someone into your sexual space.

Your sexual space was violated, but it does not have to continue to have the hold on you that it did in your adolescence. Managing sexual energy, intimacy, passion, liberation, sensuality, self-expression, self-love, and acceptance is an on-going process. Interestingly enough, it is the graduation or successful advancement through this stage of development that is supposed to lead to fidelity and adaptation to acceptable societal norms within our adult relationships.

Here, Yvette is your next letter. Be sure to fill in the blanks with whatever comes into your mind first. Don't overthink it. Follow your first mind because that is where the truth is for you.

Dear Young _____,

*I am here to love you, to protect you, and to comfort you.
Mostly, however, I am here to support you in taking your life
back. I am aware that _____,.
This left your heart broken and you were left to pick up the
pieces. Amongst those pieces laid your: _____
_____. It felt as though your world: _____
_____. You have remained stuck in these feelings
of:_____. The truth is these things did happen, but
they did not happen to you, they happened for you. These
things happened to show you that, even in your darkest
moments, you are still a beacon of light. These things happened
to help you realize that, even in times of adversity and defeat,
neither your power nor your authenticity can be taken from
you. No one can rob you of who you are. Who you are is who
you are and nothing outside of you can define or redefine that
truth. I am deeply sorry for these hurtful experiences, but you
no longer have to live or hide in the shadows of the hurt.*

*Allow me to hold your hand and to have your back. Together we
can tell our story. Together we can boldly move forward, not as
victim, but as victor. Together we can mend our heart. Together,
we can create a beautiful picture of what The Divine intended
for our life.*

Warm Regards,

_____,

And here are some new questions to think about before the next session. They are going to be similar to the previous set of questions asked, but based more closely on the issues we've just discussed. It is particularly important for you to answer these as we move into the next period. I want you to feel that you have fully shared your presence of mind during this time period of your life. So when you go home answer these questions:

What do you think about your body now?

Are you comfortable with your sexuality?

"I am starting to feel a little bit better now that I am sharing and releasing this stuff for the first time!" Yvette offered. "I don't feel guilty now, which is actually a good feeling-not to feel bogged down with so much guilt for a change! I still feel a lot of shame though."

"No worries," Yvette. "We're going to work through all of those heavy feelings and emotions as we continue to ease through these sessions. Just make sure that you keep doing the homework that I am giving you because it will play a big part in shifting your connection to a lot of your past trauma. I want to commend you right now for being so open, honest and willing to share as you release your story. You're doing a wonderful job in this healing process, so keep up the great work.

We are designed for survival, when we incur wounds our cells spring into action creating a scab; a protective hardened covering which enables the healing of wounds while shielding them from further trauma. When an experience is too much to mentally and emotionally process we have an automatic response to shift focus and consciousness to an area more within our control, and more tolerable to the psyche. Traumatic experiences are never forgotten Yvette, they merely shift to a less prominent position until we become able to process it.

Are we born with resilience? Maybe, maybe not. However, as long as we draw breath, grow and journey forward through life, we are employing those muscles that make us resilient; and just like the willow, we are perfecting our bends. We are learning how not to be broken by trials. In the journey toward self-love, self-acceptance and self-knowledge, it is important to recognize the amount of effort put into keeping us from discovering the truth about our power. Now, imagine what we could do if we knew our power and channeled it effortlessly into nurturance and guidance? We would undoubtedly set this world on fire.

So let's get you empowered and ready to passionately love yourself with fire!

Here are your new affirmations that I am assigning you to repeat out loud to yourself each day in the morning when you first wake up and in the evening before you go to bed, until we meet again, along with another handout for you to ponder. In our next session, we will discuss the impact of these assignments, emotionally and physically.

AFFIRMATIONS

Nothing in my life has happened to me, rather everything is happening for me.

I am whole and complete.

I can't control every experience in my life, but I can always choose how I respond.

The measure of my worth always comes from within.

I am worthy, simply because I exist as an expression of The Divine.

I refuse to be a victim. I am a victor.

There's not anyone or anything that can change who I am at my core.

I honor me, by telling my story in a way that is healing to me and ushers the healing of others.

I release all shame, guilt, resentment, and anger.

No matter what life deals us, we have the innate ability--
the power and skills needed to survive even the most dire
circumstances. The human spirit is resilient, and sometimes
that resilience is all we have to push us to face another day.
As long as we have the capacity to draw breath, we must
face another day. Many people would argue that strength
and fortitude are the best methods for survival however,
if this were true, the oak tree would have the capacity to
weather any storm. It does not. It is actually the willow, which
appears delicate and easily broken to the eye, but in reality
it is flexible and adaptive by divine design. The willow tree is
more likely to withstand the torrential ravages of nature long
after the mighty oak's been shredded. After the storm and
at the dawn of calm, the willow may be without some of its
beautiful sprouts, but the essence of the tree and the core of
its strength remain well-rooted.

Are we born with resilience just as we are born with our
internal organs? Perhaps, but what is certain is neither--if
left untried and tested--will maintain its strength and vitality.
Such is life. How do you get through the tempest and torrent
of your story? First, you do not give in to the circumstances.
The situations will be footnotes, because at best they are
temporary and do not define you. They are not the legacy
which will become your mark on time--how you work through
those circumstances though—this will become your life's
narrative.

The issues we face are not unique. No matter what happens
to us, no matter how it seems, it has happened before and is
in fact happening to someone else right now. But, how we get
through--that is the basis for our distinct stories. As we move
through life, there will always be someone who will attempt to
peg you with a title of their choosing, many of which may not

be flattering. Look at these as simply verbal handcuffs; they are mental vices designed to put you in, and keep you in place. Bitch, whore, slut, trick, the words are myriad but the goal is singular, to kill and maim the spirit. It is then your responsibility to never give into or give up on account of that diatribe. This is no easy task, sidestepping misogyny, insult, and injury while refusing to buy into these titles--detrimental to, yet so haphazardly flung toward women and girls.

Chapter 6

*What can I do to make you feel secure, remove all your
doubts / So that you'll know for sure that you're the
apple of my eye, girl? / Fulfillment of my dreams, time
will show the value / Of just what you mean to me*
- (Time Will Reveal – Debarge)

Oh my GOD...Music was my man. My GOD. My Daddy. My
Lover. I let music teach me, guide me, comfort me, and mold me.
Through music I learned how to love! How to dance. How to stand
up for myself. How to be loved!

My first musical love was Debarge and *Love Me in a Special Way*.
That was my song with Jason in the 80s. Followed by *Time will
Reveal* by Debarge. Then their song *A Dream* sealed the deal on
my fantasy fairytale. Debarge was a big factor in my life because
I grew up 45 minutes away from where they grew up so we would
drive to see them perform and I had ALL of their music!!!

In 1984, Kim Fields taught me how to reveal my love in a letter
with her song to Michael Jackson called, *Dear Michael*. So I spent
the second half of my 8th grade year writing Jason love letters
filled with love songs.

But by the summer of 1985, my fantasy fairytale romance with
music was officially over. Interrupted like a scratch on an old
vinyl record, by the song *Dear Yvette*. *Dear Yvette* crushed me,
because I had put my heart out there and laid my feelings on the
line just to have them returned back to me void and with a big
stamp screaming REJECTED! That's how I felt, anyway. I felt
rejected and unworthy, by all the boys.

Even though they didn't know my story, that song left me feeling
like they all knew. Alonzo knew and that was all that mattered to
me as he paraded around the weekly neighborhood parties yelling
out the lyrics to *Dear Yvette* and getting everybody else crunk to
do the same. From that point on, in my mind, they all knew that I
was damaged goods and that nobody would want me as a result of

it because the boys seemed to love every word of what was said on that album, especially that damn song!

They used it against the nasty girls and I hated it. Everybody loved LL Cool J... so who was I to stand up against that? All I felt that I could do was crawl under a rock and die because I was damaged goods. I felt worthless. Less than. No longer the girl in anybody's dream. Definitely not the girl in any fairytale.

That song lacked compassion. The compassion that a person could have for a young and obviously wayward girl! That could have been a platform or an outlet for me to finally tell somebody about what was going on with me, but instead it became a badge of dishonor and degradation.

Boy if I could turn back the hands of time, I would. If I could trade my real story in for a fairy tale, I most certainly would. Picture-perfect, a storybook ending, now *that* would've been divine. But it wouldn't... it couldn't, what's done is done. I was forever changed. Moving forward was again my only option. Life after Alonzo. It was like a story you'd hear on the evening news or some crazy shit, like that. A few years after Dear Yvette came out, Tupac released a great song called "Brenda's Got a Baby" and I just remembered how compelling that song was to get people to pay more attention to issues like incest and neglect going on in the hood amongst young girls. Tupac's song incited a movement towards helping girls like me because of its compassion. But Dear Yvette simply shamed girls like me. Just full of judgment and not an ounce of compassion. I always wondered, if the girl is a hoe, what does that make the boys who sleep with her?

I became distant and unplugged from life. I slipped into my imaginary world, where I could make everything seem good and happy. I went through the rest of my 9th grade school year pretty numb. I moved in with Aunt Trice and helped her to raise her son while she worked and went to college.

And I secretly had sex with 2 different, very popular guys from my high school. One was a high school senior and star basketball player who I met in the hallway after school one day. He already had a girlfriend that everybody knew about, including me. His girlfriend was a sanctified virgin and everybody knew that he cheated on her. I also met this guy that was a year older than me and his cousin was this handsome, really popular athlete that dated my best friend during our freshman year. She was this really cute white girl that loved black guys and all the popular black guys loved her and often used me to get to her. So by default, as the sidekicks, the cousin and I eventually began to hook up.

Because my "aunt" Trice worked and went to school until late hours, it was easy to sneak boys over without getting caught. But eventually I was caught and Aunt Trice asked me to leave, so I moved in with my friend Leslie's family. Even though I had known Leslie since the 5th grade, she and I now went to different high schools. Usually I would get up each morning and go to my high school and she and her siblings would go to theirs.

But one day I decided to skip school and hang out at her school. As it happened, an old, close childhood friend who I used to play with in the band also went to Leslie's high school. He died that day. His heart exploded while swimming under water in gym class. I was there and the fear of being recognized for not belonging in that class or at the high school, the horror of seeing his floating body, the emergency medical assistance that showed up – it was the most chaotic experience of my life! My heart races even still, reliving that experience. I was so scared and sad and traumatized all at the same time. I snuck out of the building and jumped on a city bus and went back to my school.

His funeral was absolutely crazy with so much drama and stories. That was my second funeral (after Grandma Carolyn) and the last funeral that I would attend. For months I acted as if I had never gone to that school that day because I didn't want to be found out that I was skipping school. I felt like Leslie resented me for that, so eventually I moved out of her house and back home with my mom.

Would you believe that in that time-just six months from the time I left to go live with my friends, my mom- this motherfucker had become full blown crack addict! Full blown! But she was my mother... I still loved her... and there was nothing I could do about either of those facts. I was angry as hell.

My mom was really barely living at home-damn...no one really did. It was a crack house and Alonzo was dealing right out of our living room. He didn't have to go far to get customers, neither, 'cause hell, they were all running the house with us. My mother and her damn friends were some of his best customers! That's not all either. My brother was now 'Team Alonzo'. Now Junior was his protégé—13 years old, stealing cars, smoking weed, selling drugs, going to school only when and if the mood struck him. So fucked up- I really hated this shit. There was just so much wrong with it, but y'know, I couldn't tell his little hard-headed ass shit! Just a fucking follower, little fool ass dude, running behind that no – good-ass Alonzo!

Meanwhile, mom would go missing for days at a time. So I would worry about her and sometimes get really bad feelings that she was in trouble somehow and therefore go out into the neighborhood to find her. I used to go into all types of abandon buildings or houses filled with dope fiends who would gather together to do drugs. All kinds of crazy shit happened in those places. They turned tricks for money, they robbed people and came back to these dark horrible places for refuge. They shared needles or smoked crack together in these condemned hole in the wall spaces that existed deep into the cracks and crevices of the hood. Seeing my mother like this destroyed even more parts of me. It chipped away at my core even more. I remember being so confused about what to do or who to tell or even how I could help her! So I just supported her by looking out for her as much as I could.

My resolve became to simply do the best that I can to help her through this and do the best that I can to never succumb to this kind of life for myself. Primarily because I saw firsthand that the drug infested lifestyle was not a good one. Even the parts that seem to glitter like gold, sucked! Alonzo and all of his drug dealing buddies stayed in trouble with the law. Girls who dated them stayed being passed around from dope boy to dope boy competing for the affection that was clearly being shared and rationed out by dudes like Alonzo who barely bathed their own asses, let alone truly put in the time to take care of somebody else's ass! So it created a whole bunch of babymama's and deadbeat daddy's and short term hustlers with long-term issues and that entire lifestyle was a dead end zone to me. The people in it either ended up dead, locked up and incarcerated or barely escaping with their dear life.

So I learned firsthand, that drugs are umm....bad as hell for real! And trust me I had all types of dope boys trying to get with me, but I made it known very early on that I liked the quiet, nerdy, smart boys who were more focused on making an honest living with their lives than the dudes that lived for selling dope and living that fast life. So one day I snapped! Alonzo and I had a fight that changed us forever.

This one day, he pushed me to the edge and I snapped! I was sitting at home doing homework and he kept trying to annoy me by sitting his boom box next to me and blasting music in my ear. I told him several times to stop and leave me alone. I had met a really nice nerdy guy at school whom I had invited over to help me study for a test. So Alonzo was acting a pure ass on this day! As I apologized to my friend for my uncle's ridiculous behavior, Alonzo got all up in his face talking about "whatchu gone do about it wit yo punk ass"? I immediately jumped in between the two and yelled at Alonzo to leave us alone and get out there with all of that loud ass music! Alonzo then pushed him and then hit me in the face. Something came over me and all I remember is that I ran into the kitchen and grabbed a butcher knife and then chased Alonzo's ass out the door and down the street. After that, he never bothered me again.

I really shouldn't say this, but GOOD for YOU! Standing up to him had to feel good. I'm sorry that it took the threat of bodily harm, but knowing that you had the strength to do it is an awesome show of courage. I do want to ask about your brother, though. What did you feel about your brother and what he was doing aside from being- disgusted? Sad? Angry? Scared? I'm also wondering, Yvette, where was your sister during all of this?

At that time, it was just me and my little brother. It was fortunate that my sister Faye escaped this nightmare because she got sent to Texas to live with her "dad", a man who was rumored to be her "biological" father. I think now that I was in a constant state of being disgusted, angry, and scared. Things were really bad- my house was so dangerous, I stayed away as much as possible. I wanted so much for things to be different, but I guess it was just gon' be what it was. It was a crack house, and my mom was a crack head, and my little brother was caught up—shit, it was a nightmare! My life was fucked up but that's just what the fuck it was!

It's a good thing you didn't give up. It may or may not be of some comfort, but I can tell you that this period in life is painful for nearly everyone". Angela adjusts her position in the chair, crosses her long legs, pulls her hair back, and continues. "This period in your life, the teens, deals with the conflict between your identity and role confusion. To put this in perspective, the most important question you are trying to answer is, 'Who am I?' In your case, this identity is of someone who has struggled with being loved, with loving, and with feelings of being lovable. The identity of a teenager whose mother was strung out on crack cocaine, one who-as the older sister of siblings who needed you -was unable to help them or yourself. The identity of a teenager who has been repeatedly sexually abused over several years in silence. Do you understand how these thoughts play a part in how you perceive yourself and your identity? Your recall of the past tells me that it really has felt like a shattered fairy tale and you can't clean up the mess. I want you to shift gears for a minute and tell me about a pleasant memory from this time, Yvette.

A pleasant memory?... Well, when I started the 10th grade I met this boy named *Morris*. He was quiet and a little nerdy but I thought he was very cute. He sat right in front of me in gym. We used to joke around a lot during roll call. He was a genuinely nice guy, and we flirted for a while. Eventually I had a mutual friend hook us up. We started dating and actually became close. I felt free to be myself with Morris, and I shared just about everything with him. I felt he understood me, and he *knew* me... as well as one could really know *me*. He became my best friend, and for the time we were together, we just shut the whole world out and it was just us-me and Morris. Life felt good.

Oh, that's really good. I see that your body has relaxed and your hands are not all balled up anymore. I'm pointing this out because I want you to become more aware of how your body tells more of every piece of your life story. Tell me more about Morris.

Morris ran cross-country track, and that inspired me to join the track team. I was crazy about him and wanted to spend every waking moment with him. If there was really such a thing as a knight in shining armor, he was mine. He was funny, cute, kind and considerate. When Morris got his first car and a fast food job, nothing could stop us from being together. We went to the movies and did fun stuff all summer, sometimes with other couples. We were really an item. It was an official relationship. But, while I spent my days in Lover's Wonderland with Morris, all hell was still breaking loose at home.

Back at the crack house, the police were looking for Alonzo *and* my little brother for stealing Stanley's car. I had to do something to get my brother out of this bullshit if he was going to have a chance. He just couldn't -or wouldn't- act right for nothing in that damn house. So, to keep him alive and from going to jail, I arranged for him to go live with our dad in Atlanta.

Yvette, do you remember what I was saying before about role confusion? Well, here is your example. People often see the potential future based on their experiences and then usually grow into adults who don't know who they are or what their role is. I want to point out to you the resilience and courage that you demonstrated by getting your brother out of harm's way. What I also want you to note is that you remained. We can go into that later, but I want you to see that it took a lot of strength and resolve to find solutions for your brother. That is something to be

proud of. There is a part of you that knows and has always known how to be supportive and loving. Keep this in mind the next time you want to beat yourself up about not having a perfect life. Ok? Ok. Now, back to Morris. Do you feel like your relationship remained healthy in spite of what was going on?

Morris' mom-whom he lived with- hated the idea of Morris and me dating. It felt like she spent a lot of energy trying to prevent us from being together so, we spent most of our together-time at his dad's on the weekends and during summer break. His dad and stepmother liked me and were supportive of us dating. I was able to really be a *regular* teen with Morris. There was no pressure to do drugs, have sex, or get into any kind of trouble when I was with him; we just had good, wholesome fun together. Just two big kids, clowning around having fun; going to the movies and hanging out with friends. All that fun stuff! But y'know, we each still had our own set of personal issues too. Morris was adopted and had his own struggles navigating the relationship with his mom, and me- I was living in a crack house, navigating the relationship with my own mom.

We eventually got to a place in our relationship where we began to share more and truly confide in each other. Those secrets were the glue that really bonded us, and you know what? For the first time ever, I really felt safe, genuinely cared for and appreciated in the presence of male company. Even though I can remember still wanting my dad's attention, I could finally, really tell someone what was going on in my life. Morris was that someone, and I was grateful to have him in my life. Overall, tenth grade was nice...it was blissful.

That really is a defining relationship. It sounds like you really had someone who met your needs in a way that no one else had even tried, let alone got close enough. Since you said you felt no pressure to have sex, did it stay that way?

Yvette gets up from the chair, walks over to the window, smiles and looks out.

Almost a whole year went by before we started having sex... this was big for me, considering everything I'd been through. I was afraid that he wouldn't like me or I would think... *What would* he think of me if he knew I wasn't a virgin? So, I lied to him and led him to believe he was my first.

Yvette looks back at Angela knowing that there's a question.

"So when you decided to keep the truth from him, it was an effort to prevent him from judging you? You were playing it safe, so to speak?" asked Angela.

Yvette nods her head and agrees.

"I want to put something else in your head, and you may have heard it before. Always keep in mind that whatever is judged by us is really about us. So, you were and still may be judging yourself for what happened, but you don't have to anymore. Let that marinate for a moment. OK?" offered Angela.

Yvette continues.

By eleventh grade, I was able to devise another plan to move away from home-well, the crack house. I moved out and got an apartment with one of my girlfriends who I'd known since early childhood. She and I shared similar home life experiences-so we were kindred spirits, I suppose. Moni and I pretended to be local college students and we were able to rent an affordable 2-bedroom apartment- two high school students with part-time jobs. *And*, we went to school every day like it was just another day. We were so focused. We were determined to get out of our situations and get an education. That's all we really wanted.

Morris was over all the time; he was a huge help with essentials like food and transportation. But, when Morris wasn't there... my lifestyle began to change. Now living in the heart of that college environment, it quickly became a sex fest. I had begun to develop other friendships with older male friends who also didn't mind *helping*. Morris definitely didn't know this, hell no! He would have been pissed! I know I justified it because I needed, I don't know, whatever the other friends had to give. Affection. Attention. Money. Sex. I did what I wanted to. I mean, I knew Morris was my boyfriend, but with my new older friends and new freedom, I took advantage of the opportunity. I was older and fucking around with older guys. It just came with the territory. Don't get me wrong, Morris and I were still doing our thing and, for the most part, doing it well, but there was definitely trouble brewing just below the surface in paradise.

Living on my own, in my own place, I guess this wasn't the best thing for me as a sixteen year old and definitely not the best thing for my young relationship, with Morris. I also had a huge crush on another dude, let's call him Mr. Popular. He was a senior when I met Morris and now a freshman in college. He, of course, did not give me a second look and I hated that! The thing is though, that his sister and I became good friends and I used that as my way in. I was *determined*, not to mention, insecure, and I could not and sure as hell *would not* be denied. I really hated rejection.

I remember thinking - he has some nerve! Yeah, it only ignited my fire to have him even more. And he wasn't just gonna *like* me, no, I had to prove to him and myself that I was *desirable*. I had to show him that I was the *shit*. And, so I did, by doing something stupid and regretful -I slept with one of his boys. Wrong. Fucking stupid idea, Yvette!

As a result of me sleeping with his friend, he and the rest of his boys thought I was easy, and started coming to me for sex. I guess I became 'the chick that fucks'. *If you wanna fuck, she will. She fuckin'.* Just what the fuck was I thinking? I didn't realize the picture I was painting. But I would eventually get what I wanted. I got "Mr. Popular" after *all* the bullshit I went through and you know what? Hold up, lemme grab the mic and blast this - his dick was *wack*! He had no dick game! Bottom line, the worst! Worse than lame! As a matter of fact, I can safely say his was the worst sex I've had to this very day! It really was disgusting. I felt like I would throw up every time. What was I thinking?

I was having sex with quite a few dudes, until it all came to a head. Yes, I was still having an idyllic relationship with Morris.

We would go to parties at the local college, but we were invited mostly because everyone thought Moni and I were in college, too. But I want to tell you about this one particular party because that's when everything went crazy. I took Morris, but a dude who I used to fuck was there, as well as one I was currently fucking. And Boom! My secret life and my public life had crashed! Morris walked in on one of them pinning me up against the wall. Of course, Morris, my boyfriend, came to defend me and all hell broke loose. They argued-of course, but then the other dude, the one I was actually *still* fucking went and opened his big mouth. I was busted like a motherfucker. Then some other dude jumps in and they *both* tried to jump Morris. Shit got real ugly, real quick when one of those bitch asses revealed that I had actually fucked both of them. It was crazy. Morris was so hurt. He didn't say it-he didn't have to, I knew. I fucked up- I fucked up something *so* good.

Angela let silence hang in the air for several moments. No questions. No interruptions. Yvette needed to sit with this.

I couldn't blame this part of my life on anyone but myself. My relationship with Morris was permanently damaged. What the fuck were you thinking, is all I kept thinking. But I guess I just wasn't-thinking. I remember *feeling* miserable, I was sad and felt so much guilt for hurting Morris. I begged for forgiveness, and said whatever I thought he needed to hear. I wanted him to believe in me- in *us* again. I failed Morris... I failed me, and things were actually never the same. No more innocence, no more simple fun, no more just being free. We couldn't get back to the way we were. In truth, he finally saw me for who I was... and I shattered his fairy tale.

There it is again. That fairy tale. The use of the fairy tale is to tell a story, but you have to know that everyone has their own story and it has value, too. Were you able to work things out or no?

We broke up countless times, only to get back together again, and repeat. We were officially on an emotional rollercoaster that seemed to never stop. I felt like he kept coming back for the sex, but not actually for *me*. I wanted him to love *me* again, so although I suspected that as the reason, each time he came back, we had lots of sex. I just wanted so badly for us to be OK, and I thought if we made love enough, it could be enough. Just like an addict, I was chasing the feeling of that first high-that first love, that first male friend, the one I could feel safe around, the one I could depend on.

Chapter 7

It's just the little things you do
That show how much you really care
Like when I'm all alone with you
You know exactly what to do
You put that fire inside of me
And make it more than just a dream
— (I Like It —DeBarge)

Halfway through eleventh grade, I was informed that I would not graduate on time-I was a few credits short. I had to get it together if I was going to graduate on time, and that meant I would have to attend night school, so I did. In spite of it all, failure was not an option-nope, not for me. Morris helped me get to and from night school, and although I was struggling to get back on track academically, I managed to take full advantage of time with him to get back in his good graces. Sex. Sex was *always* on the table. I felt the return of the closeness we shared and it, well-it made him happy. 'Cept, all this fucking would result in a pregnancy by the end of the school year.

Morris and I were in agreement about getting an abortion because we didn't want a baby. I asked my aunt Sherrie, my dad's younger sister, to help me and she did. So I had another abortion- done and over.

With all that you have experienced leading up to this, I can hear the distance in your retelling. It's as though it happened to you, but from a remote place with no connection to what you've shared. It's almost as if it happened to someone else. Let me ask you to do something as you continue to talk- hold your right hand on your chest. OK?

Yvette places her hand lightly on her chest and instinctively takes a deep breath.

Angela continues, "I'm having you do this so you

can be aware of your heart as you speak. All issues
of the heart get their start there-compassion,
trust, resentment, anger, grief, loneliness, hope,
commitment, hate and love. It may seem easy to tell
a teenager that they don't know a thing about love,
yet they clearly know when their hearts are hurting.
Doing things you don't want to do in order to avoid
being alone is what happens when loneliness shows
up in your psyche. Please continue Yvette."

Finally it was, the end of eleventh grade, and I was off to Miami
for the next 6 weeks. My time in Miami was memorable, but I
was ready to get home to Morris. I had to visit with my dad and
brother for two weeks in Atlanta before finally getting back home,
back to school-late-and, smack dab into the realization that I
was not the only one who spent the summer fucking around.
Morris was fucking around, too now, and I was mad as hell about
it! What a way to start my senior year. Not only was Morris
cheating, he was cheating with a damn white girl! Ah man, we
were through!

I was hanging out in the cafeteria bragging about my summer
escapades in Miami and Atlanta, fully intent on making Morris
jealous. He wasn't there, but his running buddies were at the
table right next to ours. I made sure to lay it on thick enough so
they could hear. Little did I know, the nosey old cafeteria lady
heard me, too. But what she also heard was me boasting about
how my roommate and I lived over in college town. Come to find
out she and our landlord are sisters- go figure! Needless to say,
the truth was out and so were we. Even though we paid our
rent on time every month, we were still underage. Damn! I had
to move back in with my mom. I was so *pissed*. Oh, just fuck
everybody-that's how I felt!

I moved back in with my mom in yet another place, and this time,
my mom had a different boyfriend to go along with it. This one's
name was Hill, and he was rumored to be an old pimp. Shortly
after I came back home to live with momma, so did my sister. She
was just entering high school and had returned home from Texas
to live with us again. So for a short time, it seemed sort of family-
like again, that is, until my mom started disappearing again

for days and sometimes weeks at a time, leaving her boyfriend behind with us, until he'd find her, beat her, and bring her ass back home. She was a complete mess- these days she was hardly even *sorta* sober.

At some point, Hill moved us to a different house where he kept her locked up in the house most of the time. But, she'd eventually succumb to the lure of her addiction and find her way out for days at a time again. I spent so much time and energy doing what I thought was helping her, back then-going out and looking for her, with hopes of finding her before Hill did. She was in bad shape. She had abscesses on her hands and feet from shooting cocaine. My sister and I did our best to take care of her. Again and again, we tried our hardest to keep her from disappearing. It broke my heart to see what was happening to her. No matter what we did, we couldn't fix her! We just weren't equipped. She just kept disappearing on her drug binges and her pimp boyfriend, Hill, kept going to find her, beat her and bring her home. Meantime, Morris and I managed to continue the dysfunction of our on again, off again, but always fucking relationship. And of course, I got pregnant. *Again.*

Chapter 8

And when the princess opened the door the frog came in, and slept upon her pillow as before, till the morning broke. And the third night he did the same. But when the princess awoke on the following morning she was astonished to see, instead of the frog, a handsome prince, gazing on her with the most beautiful eyes she had ever seen and standing at the head of her bed.
- The Frog Prince

This time I was 18 and I didn't need anyone's consent to get an abortion. Morris and I scraped up the funds and he took me to the clinic. This was abortion number three and it moved me no more than the first two. I simply didn't want a baby. I already had so much on my plate. Plus I vowed never to bring a child into this fucked up situation that I had to live with! So I focused on living through day school, night school, home life-Morris, my mother and her vicious cycle of addiction, all of it was just draining me, without bringing children into that equation.

I remember desperately wanting to be free-to escape, and so I did-again. This time, I moved in with a friend of the family who I affectionately referred to as my 'play uncle'. He knew my mom, he knew my story, our situation and he understood that I needed help. So I finally got some peace- a break from the stress. I now, again, felt like I could really focus on my future.

Morris and I were focused on taking the SAT and ACT because we both had college on our minds. The shift to future focus was good for us—it pushed our relationship drama to the backburner. The second half of my senior year felt like what I thought being a senior was all about. I still loved me some Morris and was happy that we were doing good. We were back to doing regular kid shit-goofy shit that all the seniors in high school were up to. We took our senior pictures together and everything. We even made plans to go to college together. We were normal teenaged lovers and I can't begin to express how happy I was for just about everything at that time in my life. But then came the monkey wrench-his mother was the monkey looking to fuck up our plans. Morris was not having that though-not at all. I did mention that she didn't like me, right?

That is an understatement. I think she hated me. I think I made her skin crawl. She was unrelenting in her quest to keep Morris and me apart and mess up our plans. But that didn't stop us. We just spent more time at his dad's house, where we were welcome.

Where was I? Oh yeah, senior year was about to end and, yes, I was gonna graduate on time! I was so incredibly proud of myself, I couldn't wait to share my excitement with my counselor, Mr. Copeland. So I went down to his office one day and while we were talking, he told me that he had been pulling for me the whole time and I realized that he didn't even know half of the story. He had noticed a change in me but he had no idea the struggles I was dealing with. Norman Copeland had been my counselor in elementary, then again in middle school and throughout my high school years. He was my earth angel! This time, for the first time ever (outside of Morris), I shared my truth- my struggle with Mr. Copeland. At first it was kind of uncomfortable doing so, because I felt so ashamed but because I trusted Mr. Copeland, I also felt free at the same time.

I remember it felt wrong on some level, like a betrayal, but I didn't stop. I told him my mother was strung out on crack cocaine, and alcohol. I told him that she needed help. On the inside I was incredibly sad for myself, for my mom—truth be told, I was sad about the whole damn situation. But, it turned out it was the best thing I could have done for her, and us, because he called the authorities. He had an obligation to report what I had told him. Yes, I put my mother in a position where prison was a possibility and a near likelihood, but GOD placed her somewhere better. She ultimately chose to get some help and go to treatment for substance abuse.

Yea, it was a relief, but at the same time, I felt like I was betraying my mom-betraying my whole family, in fact. I was telling this horrible secret. I was so embarrassed but I couldn't *not* tell him what was going on. At this point, even though it felt wrong, it felt necessary. And even though life was better on the home front, school wasn't quite over. I still needed support and thanks to Morris, his dad, and my play-uncle Reggie, I made it to graduation.

That graduation was so sweet. Morris walked the stage right before me and waited on stage after receiving his diploma while I received mine. Then, he held out his hand for me, and hands locked, we raised them high above us. This was for everyone to see that we did it together, we finished our walk across the graduation stage, together. I felt so fucking good in that moment, I was beyond elated! It would have been nice to remain in that awesome moment, because everything that lingered outside of it was anything but. There were so many real threats out there-threats to our stability, and these threats were boys. I just couldn't seem to get enough of them damn boys! Well, they were actually young men now.

I know you're wondering what was I getting from them, right? I liked sex and the attention of other men. Probably the attention more than the sex, but I just kept risking my relationship with Morris for it. I definitely got a thrill out of being wanted. Morris wasn't having this bullshit, and because of my extra-curricular activities, we remained off and on and off again.

On some level, my relationship with Morris became a thing of convenience to me. He was there when I needed him. He was a source of reliability and stability, yet I continued to disrespect him. Not for lack of love, though. You see, I think I really loved him. He really was my *everything*, but for some reason, I just kept looking for more. I started dating a dude from Detroit, and he was the last straw. He blatantly pursued me in front of Morris-no respect for our relationship at all. And, I didn't show any either. I remember feeling that stabbing Morris with my flirtatious ways just wasn't enough, I had to stab him with my promiscuity too *and* turn the knife.

The turning of the knife came when he saw us, me and Mr. Detroit together. I knew that I was hurting Morris, but, I don't know, part of me was like *so what*. Get over it. Next! I knew I still loved him, I still wanted him, but I simply would not, or could not let it show. Never let 'em see you sweat. That became my new MO, and even Morris was no exception. I think I was just one big emotional bag full of mixed up crazy. Maybe his mom was right all along. Or maybe deep down inside I thought I really wasn't good enough for him. Eventually, Morris had his fill of the disrespect, inappropriate flirtations, and the overall drama. So, by the end of the summer, just after our sweet graduation walk, Morris and I were officially done.

Yvette, let's press the pause button for a minute here; I think it's pretty safe to say that teenagers are notorious for falling in and out of love on a whim, at least, according to nearly every adult living or working with teens. On occasion, there are those couples who meet in high school and end up married for years, but none of us knows how to express love effortlessly without first going through this period you've just elaborated on.

The energy of love is extremely powerful, and although you were challenged, the emotional support provided to you by Morris was truly invaluable. He made a positive impression by continuing to love you although you admittedly felt that you weren't good enough and that showed up over and over again in the way you were obviously unable to accept or respectfully receive Morris' love for you.

Since you have been holding your chest, I've noticed you have been sharing more feelings and emotions, your communication isn't as distanced. You can take your hand down now; let's see if it changes your telling of the rest of your story. Yvette lowers her hand and continues.

Summer ended, and it was time to leave for college in Miami. I lived with my Grandma Jessie during the semester and attended the local community college. Morris remained at home and attended the local university where his mom received her degree. I called and wrote him quite a few times. I got no response. Of course this left me heartbroken. I knew that Morris was more than done with me.

As time went on and my need to hear from him increased, I was on the verge of stalking him! I needed to talk to him. Eventually I had a mutual friend deliver a message to him. *Finally,* he responded and let me know he hadn't received any letters or calls. Damn! Nobody could've been behind that but his damn mother! That shit made no damn sense to me at all. Who the fuck did she think she was?

Crazy as it seems-with me still being in the streets- I still loved and wanted Morris. Miami was good for my ego, though-too good. I got so much attention, *shit-* you would think I was a *celebrity*. It was ridiculous-dudes everywhere. Everywhere I went, they noticed this big butt and this pretty smile. I was used to attention, but not this level of attention. Sometimes, it made me a little self-conscious, but in the same breath, I loved it, soaked that shit right up. And yet, somewhere in the corner of my mind, Morris was still my baby.

I missed him and I couldn't shake the thought of him, so the first chance I got, I took my ass back home to see him. It was Labor Day weekend. I wanted to surprise him, so I didn't announce my arrival, I just went. Me and my girlfriends went to a party that we sorta' knew he was likely to attend, and he was there. Yup, his ass was there alright- Surprise! Morris was cuddled up with his new fucking girlfriend. I was ridiculously livid- I was devastated. Here I was coming to see him because I *missed* him. It hurt, like never before. I cursed his ass out! I know. I know it made no fucking sense, given what I was out there doing down in Miami. But fuck it. Fuck that! That's how I felt. How dare he?

As usual, we got over that moment, too. I loved the fact that we really could talk about anything, and that's what we did. Eventually, this led to making up and making love more passionately than I think we'd ever had before. I was just crazy in love with him, and that time, we didn't just make up. This time, we had the best sex ever and vowed to be together forever. And I went back to Miami happy as a lark.

I get back to school and I have every intention of keeping in contact with Morris, but no sooner than I returned, *Miami* becomes my new boyfriend- the one I give all of my attention to.

Yup, so much attention that my grandmother got enough of me rippin' and runnin' in and out of her house and kicked my ass out! I was homeless - but it was cool because I had friends I could crash with.

Before long I had at least 4 different dudes that I was casually dating and sexing. Crazy is as crazy does and I was doing some crazy-ass shit! There were dudes in pursuit and dudes I was pursuing. Shit, I even fucked a dude I wasn't even feeling. I still don't know why I did that shit.

From the outside looking in it would appear I was insatiable, and I'm inclined to agree. I guess you could say I was doing me and Morris was doing Morris. He had his girl and I had my 'friends'. In spite of all the fucking I was doing, Morris, had my heart, no matter what. I was back and forth home like every month for one damn reason or another-and always, ultimately, to see Morris.

"Yvette," Angela interjects....

"I want you to look in this mirror and say these affirmations:

There's no amount of love that I can get from another that will fill the void of a lack of self-love.

I no longer trade my body to feel good.

I commit to first filling myself with the good that I am.

Because I love and support myself, I attract others who do the same.

We're going to continue to use affirmations as a way to rewrite the negative self-talk and to express how you see yourself in your own story.

Now tell me what you did after all of that happened?

Shortly after returning to Miami from my Thanksgiving honeymoon with Morris, I ran into Sean. Sean was a popular frat boy on the campus yard. Woo! Sean was cute-just damn delicious! I loved me some red boys and he had a New Orleans accent too! Yvette said excitingly. Actually he kinda' reminded me of Morris, and I had a crush on him for a little while. So when he expressed interest in *me*-that was it! We chatted for a little bit, and he invited me to come up to his dorm to hang out later on. I was super excited, so I said, 'sure'. I was looking forward to hanging out with him- like I said, I had a crush on Frat Boy Sean for a little minute.

We chilled, watched a movie and talked-normal stuff, y'know. But, things quickly went crazy when Sean began to make his desire to fuck me known-forcefully. He surprised me by becoming aggressive, so I told him no...to stop. But he just wouldn't take no for an answer. He was forcing himself on me-literally holding me down, and it didn't matter how many times I told him to stop. He just would not stop! I squirmed—but it didn't matter. I contorted my body, pushed and fought-did not matter. No matter what I did to fight him off, to make him stop, he wanted what he wanted. I couldn't believe it. I couldn't understand why- why would *he*, Frat Boy Sean, wanna do this? I thought he liked me!

Needless to say, Fratboy Sean got what he wanted that night. He wanted some pussy, and by hook or crook, he got it! He raped me that night-That was rape! Fuck that! I call a spade a spade and I'm calling that what the fuck it is- rape. Right?

"Yes", Angela says " it is commonly referred to as date rape, because you knew who he was and had agreed to spend time with him, but you did not agree to be violated and I wish more women could see and understand that, too. What did you do after that?

I left his dorm so fast and in complete disbelief while I made my way back to my friend's dorm. I was so hurt-I just cried. I was confused and very sad, y'know? I felt broken and lost somehow... He tried to call and apologize later, but I didn't give him the chance. Just the sound of his voice completely turned my insides out. I wish I could have disappeared-just evaporate into thin air, but instead, I curled into the tightest fetal position ever and quietly cried myself to sleep. I was disheartened. Things just never felt quite right after that night. I was different inside now. My spirit was broken, I guess. I knew that I had reached my limit there in Florida. Miami would never be the same for me again and it was time for me to go.

I made plans to live with my dad in Atlanta, only to find out after I arrived that he was now on drugs too! I was so pissed when I realized this bullshit. I could not possibly do the drugged-out parent thing again- no fucking way. And, I had no sympathy for his bullshit because he had so much negative shit to say about my mom when she was battling her addiction. The thought of him getting high made me livid. There was no way I could stay there and deal with this shit again. I let my brother handle that shit.

I'd always wanted to go to Clark Atlanta University, so I set my goal on getting accepted. Actually, I applied to Clark Atlanta, Morris Brown, and Spelman, but I was accepted at Morris Brown. I was a woman on a mission who wouldn't be stopped. But I had to do some quick, funny math- which isn't my strongest subject- to make it work. Turns out my math was good, it was my money that was funny, and I wasn't able to cover the cost to move in on campus. Plan B: move into an apartment with some girlfriends from my hometown who were currently living in Atlanta. Perfect-we got that figured out, of course until I found out I was pregnant. Fuck, fuck, fuck!

Now I gotta figure out what to do about this baby, 'cause I still wasn't ready for no baby. I was really freaking out about this pregnancy thing. I called my favorite cousin in Miami- this shit was serious, and I needed help. She came through and sent me $300 for an abortion but instead, I put the money into an apartment. I used the money for an apartment thinking I could make the money back with my first paycheck. But sometimes no matter how well I think I plan, shit still don't work out. My cracked out daddy stole the $500 matriculation fee money my dad's brother Billy had sent me. And, as if this shit wasn't bad enough, my girlfriends reneged on the roommate situation after I'd already paid the fucking deposit!

So, very reluctantly, I called Morris. I told him about the pregnancy, and how miserable I was at my dad's. I was sick, angry, frustrated, tired, scared and broke. And time was ticking. If I was gonna get an abortion, I needed to do it soon. So, I asked Morris to help pay for it. But the thing is, he wasn't with that this time-no abortion. Morris wanted to keep the baby, and this response from him fucked me up. I threatened adoption. Of course, with Morris being adopted, I knew he would never forgive me if I went that route, but I did not want a baby! Not right now, not in the midst of all the crazy shit that was happening in my life at that time. I know I shouldn't have made the adoption threat-it was probably one of the most fucked up things I'd ever said to him-and there had been many. I just needed him to give me that money.

We argued and argued about the situation, but again, some things you just can't force. A few days later, Morris called my dad's place looking for me, and instead got my dad, and he fucking told him! He told my dad I was pregnant, that we were getting married *and* that he was joining the army so that he could take care of and support us! Man, I was steamed-what the fuck? Stuck, and fucked up, all I could do was cry. And, that's just what I did. I cried for days.

My mom, who was now clean, got involved in the situation and suggested I come home, and I agreed. She sent me a Greyhound bus ticket and, all I could think of the whole ride home was, *I'm having a baby- -I'm gonna be a mother*. I wasn't happy about being pregnant at all. This wasn't how it was supposed to be-not like this. *Everything* in me resisted the idea of having a baby, but that didn't make it any less true.

The first thing I did when I made it back home was reach out to a friend to talk all of this out. What I really needed was a shoulder to cry on. We met up for dinner, and Morris' dad and stepmom came into the restaurant. I tried to avoid them but they saw me, and, complete with touching my belly and all, they expressed their joy in the news of becoming grandparents. When we hugged, I could feel their love and support. And when they left, I just cried some more, right on my friend's shoulder.

I don't think I had any real expectations of Morris and me. I did expect that our parents would be angry or disappointed in me, so I was very surprised by how warmly my mother and his dad's family responded. But the truth is, I didn't really know if I was coming or going. I had no real expectations then because what I expected to have was another abortion and it was apparent that that wasn't going to happen this time.

Morris' dad and stepmom helped me get an apartment and Morris went into the Army. They also gave me a car, which helped me get back and forth to work. They were such a big, big help, more help than I would've ever expected. I still love his dad's family.

Once I settled into the idea of becoming a mommy, I wanted to be the best mommy ever. So I took my doctors' appointments very seriously. I never missed one. I took all of my vitamins and ate the best foods for my baby. If I was going to have this baby, I was gonna do it right. I read all kinds of books both to my belly and about my new baby. I even played classical music for the baby! Everything was going so well and Morris was doing his part, too. Away in the military doing basic training, he sent money home to help with the costs of preparing for our new baby. I was pregnant and happy now. There was absolutely nothing to complain about. I loved on the baby so much that by my eighth month, I looked like I was eating for four! Everyone seemed so happy and excited when we found out we were having a boy. The support I received from my family and Morris' family truly warmed my heart. I was grateful for the support. Who knew?

There was one person who certainly wasn't happy though-Morris' mom. She was relentless. She kept the bullshit coming and coming. Of course she didn't believe the baby was Morris'- like she was in the room with us while we were fucking. And, these types of accusations went on up until the day she laid eyes on our son. Until that day, she nagged Morris about getting a blood test. She thought the worst of me from the very beginning. She never gave me a chance.

But Morris did. I want you to briefly acknowledge how this made you feel. Not so much his mother's disapproval of the relationship. You two had real

**intimacy, even if it looked like it was just sex. One
aspect of your relationship with Morris is that
you guys shared a 'wound' and in the language of
intimacy, you guys bonded over your respective
wounds. I've heard you say that you two continued to
promise each other that you would always love and
support one another; much of it is because of those
wounds. This is why your teenaged love story lasted
for this many years at this point. The language of
intimacy is so important during this time in your life.
It's really the final developmental phase as an adult.
What you have shared is the attempt to organize your
lives based on supporting each other through such
woundedness.**

Well, I was ready to deliver, but Junior wasn't trying to make
an appearance! Hell, he should have been, he was 9 pounds 10
ounces when he did get here, and, that was 3 weeks early! There
is nothing joyful about delivering a baby- at least it wasn't for
me. Not Junior. First of all, he was breech and he was twenty-two
and half inches long! Plus, I wasn't dilating enough to make the
process go smoothly or quickly. Twenty- two damn hours of labor!
I was absolutely miserable! The doctor had to literally turn the
baby around while he was still inside of me to prepare him for
proper vaginal delivery. Can you imagine that shit? It felt like
absolute torture. And, they had to pull him out with forceps-the
most pain I have ever experienced in my life. But, on July 7, 1989
our boy was here, and I was elated. To honor his father, I named
him, Morris, Junior.

Junior was born with jaundice too, just as I had been, but other
than that, he was perfect-just perfect. I was so in love with
him-just consumed with love and overwhelmed by emotions. The
way his beautiful eyes connected with mine, the way he sat in my
arms; this was all beyond anything I'd ever felt. I realized that
I'd never known love-not like this, not until our eyes met. I can't
explain it, the experience, the intense divine connection between
my son and me. He was my golden child. It was like he came here
to teach me how to love.

It was amazing how much love I felt for him. I knew he was going to be a great contribution *and* contributor to the world and I knew *I* was going to be the best mother I knew how to be. Plus, I was eager and willing to learn the things I didn't know.

Junior was real light-skinned. He almost looked white, and he had a ball of skin attached to his left pinky finger. My mom reminded me that my siblings and I all had these extra fingers too, except we had them on each hand and ours didn't look like balls.

Everyone loved Junior, even Morris's mother. When she arrived and saw the extra ball of flesh on his hand, she joined Team Yvette! Apparently, Big Morris had the same exact thing-same hand and all. So she was finally convinced, smitten and very much in love with Morris, Jr. I really wanted to give it to her, 'cause I was still mad about how she had treated me, but instead, I welcomed her into our new family with open arms.

Big Morris-that's what we called him now-returned for a brief visit before he left for his first duty station in Germany. I was happy to have my true love back for the two weeks. We were all together now, with our new baby boy. I was in heaven, for sure. I felt like everything was going to be alright. After a few months, Morris' dad and stepmom bought a plane ticket for me to visit him, and they kept the baby. I was happily on my way to Augsburg, Germany for two weeks-ready to visit the love of my life, but I got a rude awakening when I arrived. Things just weren't the same-he wasn't the same, and I realized that I didn't like the new Big Morris. The Army had changed him.

Morris was smoking, drinking a lot of beer and talking even more shit. I didn't like it and this was not the person I fell in love with- not the cool, laid back nerdy dude I had always loved, not even close. And I wondered, *is this my happily ever after*? After handling all of the shit I'd already been dealt with addiction, I wasn't trying to put up with this shit again. But I wouldn't have to, because I soon realized that he didn't like me anymore either. I knew then it was over.

So, this is what people mean-y'know when they give advice and they say things like 'life happens, we fell out of love, things change'... but, what they really mean is just one thing- another fairytale is shattered.

> **Angela interjects: "This appears to be an ongoing theme of shattered fairy tales, Yvette. Where do you think the idea that you have about life and how it's supposed to be came from?**

I realized this apple doesn't fall far from the tree. It's not just happenstance that a green apple tree bears green apples, it's a fact. You just don't find a Red Delicious on a Granny Smith tree-imagine that. There just ain't no change up to the game-like I said before, it is what it is. People say they become what they come from. I am my mother's child, just like you are your mother's child. There are certain things you can't help. I am a product of my environment, the summation of my experiences. I am what I am. Just because I *know* to do better doesn't mean I *will* do better. That's where the hard part comes in. Self- preservation is everything. You can't get me-that's it, I'll get you before you get me... *Trust!*

Morris and I were just going through the motions. I got what I wanted, but I didn't really have *him*. We had planned to get married, but I didn't have *that*. Y'know that *I wanna get married* feeling- I didn't have that, and I didn't get the impression that he did either. I couldn't lie to myself about that. He came home for a visit months later and it was obvious to me that something wasn't right and it wasn't just his newfound love for smokin' and drinkin'. I mean, something *really* was not OK.

Like I said, we *did* the family thing-like we played the role, but I didn't feel like *we* were together. I was constantly bitchin' about *my* time; my time this, my time that. He never found time-nor made time, to just be with me. *Finally,* he said what had been haunting him – that he wasn't "ready to be a husband". After all this, after all these years- after having his baby that *he* insisted I have, this is what he had the fucking gall to say to me. Really? So, this is how you've been feeling? You got me up here in mid-fucking-air, and you drop me? Damn it, Morris!

We had broken up before-y'know... and all that jazz, but this time it felt *really* real. I felt his words inside me, it shook me at the depths of my soul; every fiber of my being ached. For a while, it was impossible to draw a breath. I couldn't believe after all we'd been through together, this would be it. This is how Morris would do me? I was fucked up. It may not have been apparent on the outside, but on the inside I was wounded, bad. I was destroyed by his rejection.

Once he returned to Germany, we still spoke a few times a week but, that was it. He was just kinda' playing me and I knew it. I'd found out that he had a girl in Germany. By then I couldn't believe anything his ass said and, I could not fucking stand him -I hated his dirty drawers! I was so embarrassed. I just knew Morris and I would be together forever. Even with all the disappointing things that I'd already learned about fairy tales, I believed in our happily ever after-I did.

Soon after our unhappy ending, I began to find ways to entertain myself, as usual. Shit-I needed someone or rather *something* to soothe this broken heart, so I resumed sexing dudes. All I had to do was walk my walk and someone would walk my way. None of 'em meant anything to me- they were just ego bandages. Hell, Morris didn't want me, so there really was nothing to hold me back from doing what I liked. Honestly though, nothing, no one could bandage my crushed heart. No one. I made the decision then to do for my damn self. Fuck him! Fuck Morris and his pretty German half-breed ass girlfriend! I didn't need his ass anyway- I could take care of me and mine, and make my own damn money. Really- just fuck his punk ass! Ooh, I was so mad! But, I took all of that anger and channeled it-I joined the Army too!

Yvette, you're at a point where you just can't seem to stop yourself from repeating the sexual behaviors you were exposed to and what you've chosen to do to self-soothe since you became sexually active of your own accord. Sounds like you have become stuck in a fixed pattern of self-belief and it's getting in the way of your ability to form healthy relationships with yourself and others. It sounds like you are reacting to situations

from a 'could, should, or must do' perspective, rather than focusing on the situation itself. I want you to keep this in mind while you talk about this next phase of your life. The more accurately that we can react to the right person, at the right time, and for the right reason, the more aware we are to any given situation.

I want you to do an affirmation right now. Here, hold this mirror before you and say the following three times: 'I take responsibility for my own happiness. 'Yvette complies and, Angela continues. Your willingness to account for all of the previous events of your life up to this point is really an excellent representation of your heart. Looking at this period of your adolescence-although I know it doesn't feel like adolescence- but adolescence goes into our early twenties. This is when we begin to shape the way we experience and have loving relationships. Your heart attracts all kinds of love and adoration, only to be brought down by disappointment from yourself, your family, and your lovers throughout the years.

Now just to tag your father into responsibility for his absence- losing him in your early years to both emotional and physical distance has impacted and affected you. I've noticed that you did not hold him accountable for anything other than the demons of his drug addiction. It could be his absence that contributes to you looking- almost incessantly- for love in all the wrong places. Fortunately, there was one person whose light shone so bright in your life that he was able to represent a more accurate feeling and acceptance of what love is supposed to feel like. It is almost as if Morris was placed in your life as a guardian angel to help protect your heart as much as possible through those tender heart years. So many aspects of how relationships are established and maintained begin to develop during this period. It is no wonder that many don't make it through this period successfully and continue to have the same dysfunctional outcomes as adults.

Yvette, please take the following affirmations along with the attached Letter to Self home and recite them to yourself 3 times each morning and night until we meet again.

AFFIRMATIONS

Life supports me in every way imaginable.

I remain free and flowing, no matter the circumstance.
Love is who I am.
There's no amount of love that I can get from another that will fill the void of a lack of self-love.
I choose to bend, but I refuse to break.
I accept my scars, they tell my story - the story of my resiliency.
I take responsibility for my own happiness.
I honor my body.
My love is enough.
My vagina is not a commodity.
No one can do it for me like I can.
I love and support myself.
I no longer trade my body to feel good, I commit to first filling myself with good that I am.
Because I love and support myself, I attract others who do the same.
My love flows from the inside out.

Dear Young _____,

*I see you searching far and wide, high and low. I feel your
hurt, I hear your cry. You are looking for love. You are seeking
adoration. You want to soothe your pain. You want someone-
anyone to make it all okay. You want someone to make you
OK. In your struggle to survive, you've learned to run on empty,
looking to others to fill you up. On your quest for love and
adoration, you used what you had to get what you thought
you needed. Time and time again, you traded your body for
temporary, feel good, counterfeit love. You did what you knew
how to do - survive. Your ability to survive such turbulent times
is commendable.*

*No more mere survival, it is time to live, and living means loving.
You were created to be love and to be loved. Your body doesn't
make you any more or less lovable and giving it away doesn't
ensure you'll receive love in exchange. Love isn't a result of
sex and sex isn't a result of love. Love is who you are and the
discovery of that love begins from within. It begins with you.
Its begins with first filling yourself up. It appears when you can
lovingly accept the person who looks back at you in the mirror.
It's found not by seeking, but by being. It is established, not in
trading yourself, but in standing firm in your self-worth and
value. It is rooted in honoring yourself as well as your body.*

*Speaking of roots, I have come to dig you up from the deep-
rooted belief that you must search outside of yourself to
experience love and adoration. I have laid new sod and a space
has been picked just for you. Allow me to reground you, this
time in my heart, where you will develop new roots in the soil of
my love. You will blossom in the belief that you are love. The love
that you are is the love you will experience.*

In Love,

_____,

Breathe in. Breathe out. Repeat. We do not have to think about taking our next breath, it's automatic. We do not have to remember to blink our eyes or, thankfully, the beating of our hearts. We rely on our bodies to function without our constant interference but, our job is to take care of our bodies to ensure these autonomous and involuntary happenings will occur.

Everyone needs water and food to stay alive, but what makes us feel alive is unique to each individual. How does one move beyond the reflex of perceived necessity? The history of your experiences may have you convinced that what is required for your happiness and peace may only be attained by external means. If you believe your happiness is contingent upon the actions and whims of others, you relinquish your power and become complicit in stunting your own growth.

The basic truth of life is we are ultimately responsible for our own happiness. Therefore, going through the actions of repeated patterns that do not bring us closer to what we desire leads only to more frustration and discord. Our egos may keep us stuck in these patterns with a belief that if we continue, or try to force the circle into a square, it will someday fit. It will not. True happiness cannot be attained until one has proclaimed love and acceptance of self. It is loving the whole self-the good and the bad-and making the necessary changes for you, not because they will make you more attractive to someone else.

You are already complete. One of the best and worst kept secrets is this: you already possess all that is required to make you happy and fully at peace. Your past is not a life sentence, it is not prophetic, nor is it a barrier forcing you to live within its limitations.

Think for a moment about the people who you feel have it most together- those who literally shine from inside. If you asked the shining, the truly beautiful people, how they made it to 'The Happy', you will quite likely come to find that the beauty you see is a manifestation of a fullness of appreciation and gratitude for the journey. There is no elusive ingredient for contentment, it is the simplest and, simultaneously, most complex task of recognizing and acknowledging your own self-worth. True love is realizing that your happiness is essential to your well-being and then allowing it to flow freely through every area and relationship in your life.

Step one: you must first recognize and acknowledge your self-worth. There is absolutely no one else who can do that for you.

Step two: forgive yourself for not honoring your truth. Repeat both steps until the only thing you feel is gratitude for your journey and unfiltered, unconditional love for yourself.

Chapter 9

*"But he has nothing on at all," cried at last the
whole people. That made a deep impression upon the
emperor, for it seemed to him that they were right; but
he thought to himself, "Now I must bear up to the end."
And the chamberlains walked with still greater dignity,
as if they carried the train which did not exist.*
– The Emperor's New Suit

I arranged for Junior to be taken care of by Morris' dad. I granted
him temporary legal custody while I got my life together. I knew
I'd miss him, but felt certain that joining the army was the right
thing to do, and quite honestly, I didn't care what anybody else
thought about my decision. I knew what I wanted and what I
needed-I got this. This wasn't about nobody but me, I thought. It's
my life and I'm gonna live it the way I fucking want to-bet that!
My mentality shifted-I was off to a crazy place. The saying *You're
just a squirrel in my world'* resonated, and I was taking all the
nuts, understand?

I killed in boot-camp-killed. After having Junior, my shape was
not as nice, but boot-camp toned me up right. I was addicted to
training, and wanted my Coke-bottle body back. I pushed myself
at every facet of basic training boot camp. Truth was, as much as
I did all of this life-changing stuff for me, I really wanted to show
Morris what I could do-that I could do it. I wanted him to know,
shit-you ain't the only one who gon' be somebody. Boot camp was
in the bag-smashed it. Now, it was time to move onto my first
duty station on the East Coast.

I continued to do what I'd always done, me. I had several different
male friends to help me lick the wounds that were left after my
breakup with Morris. Soon, he'd become just another memory-a
chapter from the past. And again, I moved forward and onward.

**Yvette, you've heard me say this before- but it may
have more context right now- the psychology of the
body teaches us that people develop character armor**

on a continuum that regulates extremes and balance. You are demonstrating the unrestrained impulses in the form of your libido-a high sex drive. Many women have stayed in relationships for far too long because the sex was just too good to give up-this is the same for you, except it's also the attention.

If we take every experience apart, your feelings of rejection-of any kind-was first horribly pacified by your uncle. Think about how you felt rejection from the kids at school and the community, then during each episode your uncle gave you physical confirmation and 'paid attention' to you - leading to more confusion and feelings of rejection. The confusing sexual abuse over the years became something you tolerated because it appeared to 'get him off your back' but only as long as you complied-until you couldn't stand it any longer.

The thing about almost all abuse is that you were likely the victim of a victim. He was a man- child who was also very clearly hurt and in turn, hurting others, and using your closeness as a cover-up. Sexual abuse and the anxiety it has caused you has manifested itself as an unconscious worry of losing control of wanting to be loved. Its manifested as an increased impulse to have sex, which you have equated to love, as a part of your survival. I don't know how much longer you continue to do this as an adult, but I want you to keep this in mind.

Shifting gears for a moment, tell me something that you did to develop yourself while you were feeling powerful and in control.

Well, for one, I developed a new creative outlet; I began coordinating events for the soldiers on the base. I was great at it, successful enough that I invited Morris' mother out to a big three-day weekend event I organized on the base to honor Black History Month. I invited her as a guest speaker but, we know why I really invited her. She actually showed up though and did her thang.

The event was a major success. I was pleased with myself. I can't speak for her though, she just wasn't on my team. I will say this much- she did congratulate me. Soon after this event, my year on the base was up and it was time to move on. I was off to Seoul, Korea, but with a two-week break between the duty stations. Of course, I went home. I had to see my baby boy.

I had a great visit -there were many admirers. Apparently they noticed me more now that I was no longer living at home and was 'all grown-up'. I was looking and feeling good these days, and the adoration was welcomed. The military was treating me well and it showed. Morris was officially an afterthought. I was so over him and his bullshit and nothing he could say would sway me in his direction. We spoke, but only about Junior, and as far as I was concerned, that was all there needed to be said.

My two-week stay at home came and went so fast. The flight to Korea felt long as hell, but once the plane landed, I realized I'd been dropped in the middle of a small slice of heaven. I was greeted by some of the most gracious and appreciative men I'd ever met. It felt like every man-I mean every man in sight- wanted to get to know me. I'd soon learn that all of the women on base there were treated like queens by all of the men. We were jewels, and there weren't many of us. The ratio of men to women was delightfully insane! There was something like ten *soldiers* to every woman and, like fifteen *men* to every woman, overall! I liked those odds. I had my pick of who I wanted, and even though this initially seemed great, I got overwhelmed at first. Can you believe that? I quickly figured out how to navigate this sea of men. Special thanks to my personal guide, Sgt. Scott. This chick would end up being my lifelong friend. She really helped me hone into the 'who to do and, not to do' of male pickings. It didn't take all that long for me to snag a cutie.

I was in Seoul for about a month when I met 'The Rock'; this guy who looked a lot like the wrestler/actor. Damn, the man was fine as hell. Anyway, he was a captain in the Army. I wasn't, but that apparently didn't matter. Rock, well, *Jamaal,* had his own place, which was a come up for me. He was fine, he made good money, and he had his own place. Jack-fucking-pot! Once we slept together that first time, I never left his place. He had a few issues

- he was an arrogant asshole, he was ten years my senior, he was insecure. But, Sgt Scott didn't like him even though I felt like he was everything a woman needed. That man was damn good to me-good. And, I loved every bit of it.

Jamaal showed me around Korea and hipped me to the shopping districts. This kind of knowledge was a huge opportunity because I started buying, shipping, and, selling stuff back at home. I had established a great rapport with the business owners there and did a few shipments of handbags, shoes and clothing for family. Then, I made a business of it. Eventually, I was designing my own line of clothing, which I had some tailors create, and then I sent the items back home to sell. I did that-I created my own fucking catalog, and sold over $100,000 in product before it was all said and done.

But-and, there's always a but-what actually happened was that my partner at home was flipping the money. She was using the money to purchase cocaine and sell it, but she got caught with the drugs. Of course this landed her in jail and she got two mandatory life sentences. Fucked up all the way around, huh? So long to that money, but the experience showed me what I could do-and that was something.

After I served the rest of my time in the Army; it was time for me to leave Seoul. I ended up moving back home mostly due to some bullshit story my mother concocted about her godmother. She told me her godmother was very ill, even going blind. Turns out, she really just wanted me to come home, so she created this scenario to play on my sense of obligation. When I got home, her godmother could see better 'n me! I'd been manipulated, again. I was so upset with my mom over this, because she knew that I had plans to move back to Atlanta. Besides, we'd already accrued a host of ill feelings from the past. Her guilt made her want to make it up to me, but I was bitter and resentful, so we argued a lot, mostly because I was angry over the bullshit of the past and at the same time jealous that she was putting her life together in a way that was allowing her to be a better mother figure to other young girls than she had been to us.

No matter how hard she worked to make it right, I just couldn't *not* be angry with her. My attitude and actions showed it all, and I didn't give a fuck! As you can imagine, our relationship wasn't good at all back then. For about a year, it was totally strained. Even a few more years after that, still no warm fuzzies. But I eventually realized that our relationship worked better from a distance.

Well I can see the positive in that experience, but it's worth noting that even while you start talking about what you did and how it worked that it still comes back to your mom. You said she was putting her life together.

Yeah, she was clean and sober, doing great things with her life and within the community but, I still had real issues with her - deep issues. One day, in a heated argument, she told me that she was sorry for all that she had put me through, but that she was no longer willing to be held captive by the guilt of her past! She was living a better life today and was willing to embrace what is versus what was. Around this time, she also decided to marry her boyfriend Hill, yes the same Hill from before. I couldn't believe it. I couldn't understand it. I couldn't get past it-or her, or him. I despised him for so many reasons, and the way he treated my mom fucking infuriated me. I mean, at one point I was so through with him I was willing to take his life. I pulled a gun on him and threatened to kill him, and in that moment, I meant everything I said to him. He'd just beaten her so fucking bad-I couldn't take it. Yes, it was the past, but I could never let that moment go. I felt like my mom always chose men over her children, and this decision was more of the same-no different from before.

Yvette paused to take a deep breath.

Angela said: I think you need to move around. Let's have you try the treadmill and just walk while you talk. I will stand right next to you.

I couldn't wait to leave my hometown, so I headed right back to Atlanta for school; back to my original plan. Once Morris Junior and I got settled, I felt better overall. I saw myself making moves in the direction I wanted to move, and slowly, but surely my relationship with my mom began to get better as well. It was getting good enough for her to feel she could ask me to help my sister Faye with her two baby girls while Faye was going through it with her drug-dealing baby daddy. I obliged, and offered to take care of my older niece Bridgette since she and Junior were about the same age and could attend the same preschool. I wanted to try and prevent my niece from having the same types of experiences I had as a child-I wanted to make a difference in my her life and I couldn't afford to raise both of my nieces, so my mom took the younger girl.

My bestie, Sgt. Scott from Korea was now living nearby me in Atlanta- and she was a great source of support! We really supported each other, because she was also raising a niece. The Rock was also in Atlanta and we continued to be an item. It was mostly off and on, but we were together. For the most part, we shared an intense sexual connection, but that was about it. He was in fact, crazy. Just like Sgt Scott warned me about in the beginning when I met him. All of my friends knew it too, and no one liked his crazy ass but me. And, that is all that mattered, he made me feel special. He had a lot of qualities I desired to see and grow within myself; that was my takeaway in the end. How did it end? I, of all people, couldn't deal with his cheating. After three years of fucking around, I had to give in and give up on Jamaal.

What I wouldn't let go of was my dream to make my mark in the fashion industry. I started attending Devry University for fashion. Silly me, how could I have known Devry wasn't a school for fashion? Plans thwarted, and again, I felt wronged, betrayed and lied to. It was likely my own dumb ass fault for not conducting my own research, yet I still felt lied to and misled by the school's recruiters. I wasted a year of my time, effort, and money, for nothing. This letdown added fuel to the angry blaze already roaring in my spirit and this meant nothing good-not for anyone, not even me.

I'd already been a closed book. I shared very little, and those who thought they knew me were likely mistaken because I never let anyone get that close. I generally held everything on the inside, and even though I talked a lot, I rarely, if ever, spoke the truth. I lied by omission. I didn't just flat out lie, I just didn't tell the truth. I played games. I came to realize that my only true obligation of love and loyalty was to the two small children I was raising. I gave no fucks about anyone else or their feelings. I was over the niceties. I was over being the 'good' picture perfect painting. Love me or hate me, but I sure wasn't gonna be a victim again-not me. No matter what, this time I was out for the taking and it was motivated by revenge. Not necessarily avenging anyone or anything but everyone- everyone was on the table for the stake and take.

This sounds as though you're acting on impulse again, lashing out with destructive anger at yourself and others. Let me ask you this: What do you see as valuable?

Me. After Jamaal, I decided whoever I dated would have to *pay* for my attention. I was valuable-*me*. And, Atlanta, full of eligible, successful black male professionals-they were my target group. *Y'all want this big butt and a smile? Well, it's gon' cost ya'!* I met several potential victims, I mean, candidates, Yvette laughs. I had my choosing. There were three guys I entertained with the sole purpose of financial exploitation. They were Chris, 'D', and E-Money, and I dealt with them in that order, respectively. Poor Chris. Perfect dude, I thought. Everything about him was right. He was a former professional baseball player with money in the bank. We had a great time. This lasted a year, give or take. And, his sex game was great-the bomb. All was going well, that was until I found out about his six kids and five-*five* Baby mommas. Yeah, that was a problem for me. No matter how good he looked, or how I looked at him, Chris just wasn't gon' work. He couldn't give me what I really wanted. I wanted to be a trophy. I still wanted the fairy tale I was sold on when I was a little girl. I wanted someone to take care of me, and I believed that I had the 'qualifying look' to get what I wanted. I knew I was 'that chick', but Chris- he just had too many damn kids. There was no way he could take care of me and mine-not the way I expected, nor the way I desired.

Well, what can I say, it was on to the next. Now it was 'D'. 'D' was my personal teddy bear. Lord, the booty done did it again!

I snagged me a jewel. He was cute, he was famous, and he genuinely liked me. We were hot and heavy from the start. We had sex the first day we met, and became inseparable. Junior and my niece were away with family for the summer so there was nothing stopping me from getting all that I felt I'd deserved. 'D' had a way of spoiling me and of course, I was down for it. We balled out! We partied nonstop. Hell, I met him at a club- Club 112. Man! That place was the shit. You could meet a celebrity any day of the week, and that's just what I did. 'D' was a professional football player. Money? Check! He fit the bill to pay the bills, and the great sex was a bonus. But, after about 3 months, that flame was out too. The summer ended and I couldn't continue to ball out with two small kids at home. And, that was fine. I was feeling good, no complaints. I was loving my life.

Well, soon after 'D' came E-Money; he was a lawyer and the fact that he had famous clients was a turn- on. Besides, I thought being a lawyer was something to aspire to. This made him seem like the ultimate come-up. A lawyer, and he wanted me-the thought alone was orgasmic. 'E' and I had some good times. There was this one time, when we were all out and a girlfriend dared me to strip. Quiet as it was kept, I thought I had what it took body-wise; so I took on the dare. 'E' cosigned the idea and well, that was it. I went to Club Nikki and applied for a waitress position - one step at a time. I was crazy, but not *that* damn crazy. I knew well enough to get my feet wet before I dove in. But, when I turned in my application for the waitress position, the manager was like, 'Take your clothes off.' Just rather matter-of-factly, he said, 'If you gon' work here, you got to be fine.' Initially, I thought, what the fuck, but what I actually said was, simply, 'No.'

That made no sense to me. It was quite obvious that I was fine. Shit, he could see that with my clothes on. As far as I was concerned, this dude just wanted to see me naked! But he was serious, and at some point in our conversation, he said some shit like his girls' bodies had to be stretch mark, bullet hole and, stab-wound free. I felt completely disrespected. Fuck! I was applying for a bullshit waitress position, and all of *this*? I walked the fuck out, but first I stopped in the restroom to get my nerves and a plan together. I had taken this on, now what the fuck do I do? I knew I was fine-that wasn't it, it's just, this shit kinda scared me.

I was uncomfortable as hell!

My girlfriend, the one who came with me for support, met me in the restroom. She was like: 'Do it! I got your back-trust.' I knew she did, and I knew I could trust her word. Crazy Jamaican chick. She was crazy for real! So, although I was super nervous, I did it.

The manager seemed pleased as he asked me to turn around. I felt like meat. I didn't like being on display like that. It was insulting and degrading, but I did it anyway. But y'know, through all of the mixed feelings, when he said, 'Damn girl, is that all you?'-y'know meaning my ass, I kinda liked it. It was just weirdly humiliating, yet flattering and exciting all at the same damn time. I liked attention, but I don't know, being in that position, well that was kinda awkward. I got the job, but still.

I started working at Club Nikki's the following week. I was embarrassed and didn't really want any of my male friends to see me waitressing / stripping there so a good friend promised to keep them away for me on the nights I worked. When I showed up to work- get this- I had to *pay* to work! Dude at the door was trippin', but he was serious about me paying him my money to work there! What the fuck kinda' bullshit is this? I call for the manager to straighten matters out and he said I had to pay too! Well, ain't they just full of fucking surprises? And it didn't end there.

Shortly after I got all dolled-up in my waitress get-up, the manager had another one for me. Surprise! I was, apparently, not hired to waitress, I was hired to dance. 'You dancin', now go get dressed.' And, just like that, I was a stripper. I mean, I guess I had a choice. I guess I thought- dance or be embarrassed. That wasn't much of a choice. The one thing I learned fast from one of the other waitresses who sorta' trained me-the manager-yeah, he was a big ol' asshole. I'd been put on. It was in my best interest to do what he said. And I did, I got my ass in line. I didn't take much time to think about it, I just jumped into auto-pilot, took down three shots of tequila to get my head right, and took my ass to the floor. Showtime!

In hindsight, I had no idea how hard this would be at the time I took on the bet. The truth is, it really took a lot of balls to walk out on that floor when everything in me was saying *no*. Before I could turn around twice, I had my first dance request. One song later, I was butt-ass naked. I was out there in front of all of these men, shaking my ass and acting like it didn't even faze me. Yes, this time I was actually, literally, using my body in exchange for money. Again, I like me some attention, don't get me wrong, and I could and would have sex in a heartbeat with zero reservations. But this, *stripping*, it was asking me to expose myself in a whole 'nother way.

Here comes another request for a dance at the same damn table. This was some dumb shit, if you ask me. They had money to spend though, so gon' and spend it on me, it's all good. Before I finished what seemed like the longest damn dance at the same damn table, I felt a tap on my shoulder. It was the other waitress, the one who was supposed to be sorta' training me. 'Girl, somebody requestin' you in the VIP room.' 'Me? What the hell? I started making my way to the VIP room as ol' girl filled me in on just how much money was to be made on these special VIP performances. "Girl you gon get paid tonight" the waitress smiled as she high-fived me. No sooner than I stepped into the room, someone took my hand and directed me to the couch where my customer sat and I danced for 3 damn hours. I took breaks, I think, but they were real quick cuz I wasn't sure that was even allowed. Anyway that one dance, for that one man yielded me over 1,700 dollars- my first night. Shit! I couldn't think of a better way to start my stripping career. I'm not gonna say I was hooked, but I was most certainly flattered that, *Mr. Sex You Up*, a major recording artist, hand-selected little ol' me with the big ol' booty! Bam! Damn, the booty done did it again.

I lasted a total of one whole week stripping, I just couldn't stomach it. That shit was not in my lane. The truth is that I wanted out soon after I'd gotten into that lifestyle. From what I heard, most strippers start off uncomfortable, and soon after, they get into it, or they get into whatever gets them into the mood. I'm not knockin' them, but I never got over the discomfort *or* "into it", as they say. At least not without more alcohol and I saw so many chicks using drugs which was my ultimate red flag that that shit

116

just wasn't for me, not at all. But, I did learn some things from the experience- another takeaway.

Well, it's a good thing that you were able to figure this out before any real damage could be done to your self-esteem. Like you said earlier, self-preservation was important to you. Just listening to you talk about the men and how they were not really going to give you what you needed but at the same time taking everything that they had to give in terms of money and sex but none of the men knew about each other or their roles in your life. Apparently, you used a great deal of energy taking on your many roles -and energy spread thin by involvement in so much that you never had a chance to stop and smell the roses. I can see the effects of repression as a defense mechanism. Just by pretending that you are over it all and the past didn't exist.

The hard part of all this is understanding that what happens or is done in your mind, also happens in your body. All of the attention that you 'paid' to keeping your body desirable and the effect of having the men 'pay' attention. I want to connect this to something physically tangible to make this point. Tell me about something that was going on with you physically during this time.

The only thing I can think of is, I was physically dealing with a ganglion cyst on my left wrist. It initially showed up when I was in high school, then it reappeared in my early twenties, only bigger. During the second removal, the surgeon had to go down to the bone causing severe damage to the joint and surrounding nerves. The wrist overall is still weak to this day.

Ok, that's a perfect example. Let me explain some of this connection. The psycho-emotional connection of the cyst is to the heart chakra. This area is connected with the emotional power of love. In the early parts of your adulthood, you were challenged with keeping a steady emotional climate which would allow you to act with self-care and self-love. Your fear of not having the love of your boyfriend caused the attempt to protect yourself emotionally by physically pulling your hand away from receiving unconditional love in the form of a cyst. The involvement of the biological structures interestingly have no 'official' known cause and even my basic research indicates that most patients are female. We already know that women experience more heart disease and breast cancer, too. Both are related to the heart chakra.

Come down off of the treadmill and do this one thing with me before we close the session. I want to have you do some bodywork to help balance the emotional material in your body. The physical exercise of 'thumping your thymus' is literally just a gentle tapping of the chest at the breastbone. The thymus shrinks as you age but it's a part of the immune system and, an energetic part of the chakra system. I want you to think of it in terms of immunity and helping to regulate some emotional material.

Do this with me now, just light thumping. Imagine that you are balancing your emotional states and stimulating your immunity to invaders or things that can hurt your heart. I want you to do this at home while you say these affirmations:

AFFIRMATIONS

Happiness is a choice I make each day.

My willingness to forgive myself and others frees me from a binding past.

Every experience is a lesson The Divine would have me to learn.

I am happy, not because of what others are to me or what they do for me, but because I am happiness.

In every moment lies a wealth of happiness and love; I am now willing to see it.

Today I choose to tell a different story, one of self-love and self-acceptance.

I am kind to myself, I am in love with myself, and I am happy as myself.

I accept full responsibility for my happiness.

My vagina is not a commodity.

I completely move out of the past, leaving all emotional baggage behind.

True happiness is an inside out experience.

I am willing to do things differently and see people differently.

Chapter 10

You're a back-seat queen, a elevator pro

*A high-powered body makes your Levis grow See the
stories I've heard, they could amaze
I heard she did it on a motorcycle back in the days So
calm down freak, get a G.E.D.
That's a General Education on Decency One day you'll
see, and agree with me
unless you're gonna be a freak until you're 93 For you
there's no fee, everything is free
This is from me to you, not you to me*

*Every night is your night, your leather pants are tight
You try to shake your butt with all your might
I don't really wanna dis nobody*

You might think I had a little too much Bacardi

*But that's not the problem, the problem's Yvette
     -Dear Yvette, LL Cool J*

Hi Angela. I brought something that I wrote in my journal after
our last session with me. Can I start this session off by sharing it
with you?

Absolutely Yvette. Please do! Angela responded.

Yvette walked over to the microphone and began reading the
entry from her journal:

*Change occurs without our consent. Some changes are abrupt
and seemingly without origin, while others happen as a result
of actions which may or may not be reflexive actions to past
incidents which could have been avoided. You meet the same type
of romantic partner over and over, and have a similar outcome.
This is never about them, it is always about you. Everyone
wants the fairy tale, the perfect everything— life, mate, finances,
career. As children, we are taught to believe in magic . We are
taught that love is magical. We are taught that this magic exists*

through fairy tales, like Cinderella, Snow White and the host of White knights; whether it is through the slipper that fits perfectly or the kiss that awakens us from a slumber. How do you get to your perfected reality if you are chasing someone else's fantasy? How does perfect happen? If you have never seen it, how do you recognize it? Would you recognize it?

When you get on a rollercoaster, you know the dips and curves are coming and in anticipation you brace for the expected fall. When life throws a curve, there is no warning, and how you react—negatively or positively—will determine not only the outcome but your posture after the outcome, as well. Will you make decisions based on past reactive tendencies? Or will you take possession and ownership of your life and make the decisions based on a different and desired outcome? It is easy to do the same thing, the same way and know what the outcome will be, even if it's not the desired result. We are all equipped with a full arsenal to navigate this life, there is no situation or circumstance which we encounter that we have not been divinely given the answer. When we are continually faced with the same issues and predicament, and our knee-jerk responses are the same, be prepared because the universe is a consistent and insistent teacher and will continue to place the same test on our desks until we get the answer right. It takes a moment of selfish clarity to decide that you deserve your fairy tale and concentrate your courageous efforts upon taking the steps to create your reality. When you become resolute about what you need for your perfected life, it will come and you will recognize it.

Life is based on the laws of science and, fortunately, the rules are the same for us all; we attract what we reflect. You don't have to throw your fairytale away, but for now, put it up on a shelf and save it, for entertainment purposes only. It is time for you to write a true love story.

True love is like a coming of age story; it is growing up and accepting responsibility for your love life. It's understanding that it all starts with you. It means being your very best self, just for you. Then and only then, will you receive the love you've hoped for, dreamed of, and wished for. They may not be a heroic, knight in shining armor, or dreamy princess, but they will be your matched reflection.

Taking the courageous steps to create your authentic reality will be better than any mythical happily ever after.

The things we say, the games we play, the things we do to get in our way. Karma is karmic. You know how it's been said, 'What goes around comes around. What you do comes back to you. Do unto others as you'd have done unto you.'? Well, you can't get mad if you're fucking around and you end up getting fucked. You can't get mad if you're hustling and you end up getting hustled. You can't get mad if you're on the take and you get taken. You can't get mad if you're a liar and you get lied too. You can't pick and choose the karma due you. Karma is a motherfucker. Play with fire and you're gonna get burned... I wish I'd have listened then, but it's a lesson learned. I guess I got caught up in the allure of the power of the panties.

I see that the affirmations or some real reflection has happened since our last session. That's great work Yvette. That's such a true statement – "Power in the panties", because there is so much! And really women need to learn how much power they actually have. Think about that for a minute. Only you know what kind of panties you have on, not unless you choose to share that information with someone. And we have different kinds of panties that bring us different types of emotional connections. We have our period panties, our everyday panties, our sexy panties, our going to work panties... and we psyche ourselves up with just that little piece of fabric! Our panties play a huge role in supporting our mental and emotional connection to our self-worth and confidence. Even when no one else knows what kind of panties we have on but us!

Ok, since we're talking about power, tell me what you thought you'd accomplished with that power after stripping.

Well..."E" was *not* impressed with my so-called success story at Club Nikki's because he felt that me dancing for the average Joe or a hood pop star was beneath my potential earnings. He felt that if I was going to offer myself in that way, I needed to be more upper echelon with it, put a higher price tag on it, become more of a private dancer, if I was going to put myself out there like that. He was even more convinced that I could make some real money from dudes in the upper echelons because, as he said, at the end of the day, dudes are all the same – they all like to see beautiful women, it's just that some of them have more money to spend on it! It seems I wasn't the only one who saw this ass of mine as a commodity. At this point of my life, I was still willing to take any and all men straight to the bank.

My best friend, from back home, Connie, and I had to be the stupidest chicks on earth. We used to have ongoing discussions, actual debates, around which of us had the biggest ass. That's just crazy. Honestly, I think she had me beat, but I wasn't mad. It's just, who does that? We were so young and so damn dumb. Anyway, as far as stripping, I was completely done. Besides, I could still make money with my looks and this ass, and had offers literally walking up to my front door. All I had to do was a little shake or two.

Well one day Connie proposed to me this opportunity to make some quick extra money. I believed her to be my best friend and my road dog. But after this experience, I could have strangled that chick. She and one of her friends who worked as a radio personality at a popular radio station in town, set up a private bachelor party for the three of us to dance at. The keyword here is us, we were all supposed to dance! But neither of them raggedy no-good tricks showed up! Connie did this kind of shit too often- backing out of shit at the last minute and not telling me. I don't know why I trusted her ass in the first place. She just disappears—ghost-and then the scary trick doesn't answer her phone. This is what she did the day of the bachelor party. And, when I did finally get her ass on the phone, she told me it was just gonna be me and her friend, the one who set the whole thing up. She led me to believe that chick was there already, so I went on.

When I arrived, I was the *only- fucking-female!"* There were like, thirty, shit maybe *forty,* drunken horny dudes, and here I am the only female. They were pulling on me and everything. I hurried up and got the fuck out of there, quickly. I just told *somebody* that I was going to get the other dancers and I left and never went back. That situation felt wrong and I just couldn't see any way that it might have turned out right. I left that scary heffa a voicemail message and I cursed her out. She was wrong, and I didn't fuck with either one of them fake friends like that no more after that night.

A few days after this happened, Mr. E-Money and I were chillin' at his crib. When I told him what had happened, his response was basically that I was fucking with the wrong types of chicks and he insisted that I let *him* hook me up. He claimed to know people who hired high-end dancers on the low. He really was good for my ego and self-esteem. He thought I was the shit! In his eyes, I was so sophisticated. I don't know if I believed it, but his feelings about me were enough. I don't know, I guess I was just open to get in and willing to use my sexual power wherever I fit in.

A month or so later, he booked an opportunity for me to prove my worth. An old frat brother of his, who just also happened to be a judge, was having a private party in his penthouse and wanted a few girls to come and dance. I would have to drive to South Carolina, but that was cool. E-Money made his friend's party sound really good, and it was out of town, which to me made it sound even better because I didn't want anyone in Atlanta knowing my business like that. So I was excited and also a little scared, but I trusted E-Money. All the shit he talked, hell, I knew I was gonna make some good money with no problems. And I really needed the money because my day job that I had worked for two years as an admin temp at an engineering firm was coming to an end.

The plan was to have 'E' escort me to the party, and I liked that idea because I felt comfortable knowing he would be there to protect me in case things got crazy. High end or not, people are people, it don't matter the class, you have to be careful. Anyway, when the time came for us to go, as my luck would have it, 'E' couldn't go with me for some reason or another. So I went by myself, although he was on the phone with me the whole time as I drove to his frat brothers penthouse in South Carolina. We didn't really talk about anything. It was just a comfort to me to have E's support, which showed up in the conversation as a lot of do's and don'ts! Especially that I was *not* fuck anyone, *not even* the judge.

This kinda' got on my nerves because it seemed insecure and jealous, and quite honestly out of character for 'E'.

When I finally arrived, I could see what all of the worry was about. Damn, that judge was fine! But, something wasn't right. I was the only other person at this party! "E" was still on the phone with me, just kinda listening to the judge and me talking about nothing. When he got off the phone, I became a little concerned about being there alone. But right after that thought, there was a knock at the door and a much younger girl came and joined us. He introduced her to me, like a gentleman, and offered to make me a drink. Then I chilled on the sofa while he and the young lady stepped away.

I was feeling much better now that I had a drink. I was starting to relax when I all of a sudden became a little light-headed and started feeling a little weird. So I went to get up and was about to go use the bathroom, when I realized that I couldn't! My legs felt like rubber! They were numb, I couldn't feel them; I couldn't *barely stand* never mind, walk! I felt very dizzy and fell back onto the couch. I started to panic. I was really scared. I remember thinking *what is wrong with me?* and then I just blacked out. When I woke up, I was groggy, in a fog-like haze, but still on the couch. I was laid out. But, in my last memory, I had on all my clothes, and now all I had on was an oversized t-shirt. I was nearly naked and the judge was all in my shit, between my legs eating me out! What the fuck? I couldn't get focused and there was no pleasure in any of this for me, I was just scared as hell! I was struggling to piece together what was going on. I was certain that I had had all of my clothes on. I didn't remember taking off anything but my shoes, and as my recollection became clearer, reality set in and I fucking lost it! I started yelling "You shady motherfucker you drugged me!" I was slapping him and screaming for him to get away from me!

I was freaking out, screaming as loudly as I could. I couldn't feel my legs to get away, so it's all I could do. My mind was clear enough to react, to understand that this shit wasn't right, but my body wasn't. I thought I was going to die and I started to pray for strength. I was praying to make it out of this situation and back home safely to raise my son. I wanted to live. I have never, ever in my life experienced anything like this, where I had no control over my body- well, at least my legs. The judge was trying to calm me down but that just made things worse. I did not want him to touch me. He made me cringe. I just wanted to get the fuck away from him, but I couldn't move. I was panicked and paralyzed, and my mind was racing. I couldn't process anger or sadness in that moment - it was all fear, and I was fighting for my life. I was so fucked up.

Luckily, the young girl from earlier came in the room and caught him in the act. She started screaming and ranting and accusing him of whatever, I can't quite recall. All I know is he got off of me. I just kept trying to move my legs while she went on; angry as hell. From what I could tell, she was under- age and was threatening to tell her mother about their relationship. As she reached for the phone, he snatched it out of the wall and then snatched her little ass up and took her back out of the room. Soon after, she was coming after his ass with a knife! Oh my fucking God, I thought. This was really getting crazy! I prayed and prayed, for help, for guidance, for protection. Fuck! I didn't know what to do, I just prayed. I didn't say a word or make a sound, I was just there on the couch watching it all go down around me like a fucking movie.

I have to get it together and get out of here, I thought. Luckily for me, my car keys were there with my purse right in front of me. This situation was moving faster and faster and getting scarier by the minute. This psycho bitch slashed the judge's arm just as he tried to close the door to the bedroom. I couldn't believe this was happening. I didn't take my eyes off of them for a second though. I thought if I could get to the balcony, I'd be good. I was starting to regain feeling in my legs and some control. I slid off of the sofa, grabbed my purse and keys, and then crawled towards the balcony. They were so caught up in their melee that neither noticed me as I made my way down the fire escape. There must be a God.

I have no true recollection of how I got to my car and in the sketchy details, only remember being awakened by the sound of a car ramming into the building's trash dumpster. It was the young girl from the penthouse.

I can't explain what really happened next. All I know is, sometime later, I woke up on the side of the highway with bright lights beaming through the back window of my car and a stranger tapping on the driver's side window, asking if I was ok. I was so afraid, all I could do was bawl. This whole ordeal had taken a toll on me. I was shook at my core. I don't remember when or how I got there, I just know I pulled myself together enough to drive and drove to the first exit where I parked at a gas station and called 'E'. I needed to talk to somebody who didn't require explanations as to why I was in South Carolina in the first place. Plus, this was his idea, his setup and, his bitch-ass friend.

As I replayed the night to him, I cried profusely. I was attempting to explain, as best as I could, what had happened. I must have sounded crazy or something because I could hardly speak, the way my mind was racing. No matter what I said or how I said it 'E' failed at understanding me. At times, I felt at fault, like I was defending myself to 'E'. He wasn't sensing my needs or connecting the dots between my tears, my confusion, and my inability to communicate. It didn't click for him that I had just been in trouble, it was so infuriating. Instead of consoling me, he began to argue with me. Accusing me of sleeping with his frat brother! I hung up. *I mean really! I was just fighting for my life at your friend's penthouse and this is what you have for me?*

I was too through with his ass. So when he called back, I didn't answer his phone call, and it was in that moment, as I sat in my car, feeling alone, frustrated, and misunderstood that I heard the news on the radio. My favorite female singer of all time, Phyllis Hyman, had been found dead- suicide. Depression. She'd lost her long battle with feelings of being unloved- by men. Oh God, I cried so hard. Snotting, coughing, beating on the steering wheel and yelling "WHY???". Eventually though, I knew I had to pull myself together and make it to Atlanta. So I collected myself, my thoughts and more prayer than I have ever engaged and I made my way. At some point on the drive, it came to me. I got it! Stop with the bullshit, Yvette. Go home and focus on raising your baby boy! I knew then, that if God would only see me home safely, I would stop all of the extra, dumb shit I was doing and put all of my focus on my child. Phyllis didn't have any kids, but shit, I do! So I gotta get my life together quick and just do the right thing, y'know? – Yvette gestured with her hands opened.

I started my car and headed straight back to Atlanta. Alternating between prayer and thanks, I drove and drove. I have no idea what happened to the judge or the young girl after I left South Carolina, but I do know this-it's by the grace of God alone that I am here right now.

Once I reached Atlanta, the first place I stopped was 'E"s. He shut me down immediately. He refused to let me in, refused to listen. All he kept saying was that I had slept with his sleazy-ass friend. He knew none of the horror, the things I'd been through. Rejected for something I didn't even do, I left there in tears. By the time I made it home, it was six in the morning and I have never felt more blessed and fortunate to walk in the door of my own home. I was exhausted and incredibly grateful to be alive. I headed straight for the tub. I felt filthy, through and through. I sat in the tub for a while, just thinking. I knew I had just escaped death. Somebody could have found me dead just like they had found Phyllis Hyman. God shed his grace on me and I wasn't gonna take it for granted. I never cried and prayed as much as I did that day, into the night and following day too. When I laid down for a short nap, I had one thing on my mind - church. I got up, got dressed, and took my ass to church. I needed it. It was necessary that I be forgiven, that I be surrounded by and filled with the spirit. I sought repentance and replenishment.

Phyllis Hyman was gone. That very thought brought me into the moment of clarity I needed. I was eternally grateful to be alive. Tears streamed my face as I sat silently. In fact, I cried almost the entire service. I was so happy to be alive and so repentant for going to South Carolina. What happened was a result of me doing the wrong thing. I got what I deserved, but I was also shown grace and I knew this. I needed the prayers of the church, and when the pastor asked if anyone needed prayer, I walked down that aisle crying and begging God for forgiveness. When I left church that afternoon, I still felt dirty, and went home to take another long, hot bath. Afterwards, I went to sleep and waited for the sitter to deliver my heart to me -my love, my son.

And before you even ask, no, I didn't call the police; I wouldn't know what to tell them. But, as for my mindset, I had a new perspective on life, slow and easy. I kept a low profile, well, a low profile for me. I was still who I used to be but I made a few adjustments. I had a boyfriend for a time, but when it didn't work out, I chilled hard solo dolo, y'know, alone, for a minute. I wasn't all over the place doing the extra shit. I mean, I was dating, but not that often. What's funny, well not really so funny; but eventually I slipped backed into my old pattern. I met a guy and on the very first night we met, I slept with him. We dated for about 3 months or so and I found myself in yet another life threatening situation. I guess a hard head really does make for a soft ass, 'cause as a result of "playing house", I was pregnant again.

Out of the blue, one day though while I was working at a new job, I found myself in immense pain, pain like I had never known before. I had to be rushed to the hospital, where I found out that I was 8 weeks pregnant, and this time in my tubes - it was ectopic! This was a serious complication, and I had to have emergency surgery if I was going to live. Drama, drama, and more drama. Did they mean I actually could have died that day too? A-fucking-gain? Why me Lord? What the fuck was it about me where these situations seemed to keep repeating? I had had about enough of these brushes with endangering my life!

"Tubal pregnancies and spontaneous miscarriages are energetically the body's way of saying that now is not the time, and speaking from the perspective that the energy of that embryo had a very short assignment on this human plane. How did you get through it?" Angela asks

I didn't bounce back from the surgery well, at all; I spiraled downward into a deep depression. I got to the point where I lived in darkness, twenty-four seven; I didn't answer my door or phone. I talked to no one, I went nowhere. I didn't feel like doing anything-not even living. I felt like there was a part of me that had to die. How did I get here? I was in a self-imposed prison. How did I become so unlucky in love and relationships? Why me? I was in the 'woe is me' phase from hell. But deep inside I knew it was time for me to figure out a way to live differently.

Due to my frazzled state of mind, I sent my son to live with my sister back home. Blessed that she could return the favor until I could get it together. It took about eight months for me to come out of this funk, this depression. At first I wanted to just wallow in it. But, as I started to heal, I eventually allowed others in, and this helped a lot. For one thing, my dear longtime comrade and Army buddy, Sgt. Scott, sent a friend of hers to check on me during my darkness, and this young lady, Wanda, who I really didn't know, took it upon herself to get me out of the house and back into the game. It was Wanda who invited me to the Essence festival in New Orleans. That ruse pulled me into her web of healing. That act, through her and for me, was certainly of God. I don't think she understood how life-changing this would be for me. Even I had no idea. I had every intention, initially, of telling her to just leave me the fuck alone. But, I could tell that she wouldn't take no for an answer! So, off I went, to the Essence Festival, broke, depressed and lured by the impassioned pleas of a stranger.

The Essence Festival was life-changing. I met Iyanla Vanzant-Iyanla freaking Vanzant. That would have been enough but no, it just kept getting better. Wanda purchased two books for me, *The Best Kind of Lovin'*, by the amazing author Dr. Gwendolyn Goldsby-Grant, and *Faith in the Valley*, one of Iyanla's best sellers. I was blessed to meet both authors after they spoke at the festival. I spent the next few days waking up, spiritually. I did a lot of crying, laughing, and reflecting. I realized that my journey wasn't so bad compared to some of the stories I heard there at the empowerment conference within the festival and, I believed that if those people could change their paths, then so could I.

The life changing speech for me came when Johnny Cochran unexpectedly showed up with former Black Panther Geronimo Pratt at the empowerment conference. Being in their presence was amazing. The atmosphere was electric, the energy so thick you could feel it. All eyes were focused intently on them as they spoke to the audience, and I was seeking a connection with every word that came out of their mouths, soaking up whatever offering they had to share. I remember that being a very tear-filled day. I had never experienced anything like it before. This was some good shit and I felt like I was supposed to be there. I was incredibly grateful for my comrade's persistence because I needed that!

I made a conscious decision to stop self-pitying and change my life. Because if Geronimo Pratt could endure 27 years of wrongful imprisonment and change his life, my shit was nothing. I knew I wanted something different and I now felt I had the power to pursue it. With money that I borrowed from Wanda, I purchased a few more tapes and CDs that I thought would help me along the journey. I went back to Atlanta, equipped with the tools to make the changes I sought. Over the next six months I ingested, digested and tested the contents of the purchased materials. I had an instant connection with Dr. Grant, the author, so much so, I made her an honorary Grandmother in my spirit.

Eventually, I would begin asking the questions -via journaling- that started my healing. Journaling would give me clarity and a voice. I was beginning to see the light. And what Dr. Grant provided me in the pages of her book enabled me to spot or prevent molestation and to foster a better, more protective relationship with my children.

> **We are going to have to end this session, but I am going to note that you have started to gather some of the many tools to help you process the things that have happened to you. I think that you could probably benefit from having a massage before next week, if you don't already get regular bodywork. That's your homework, and you are to set the intention to leave whatever is emotionally hanging out in your body on that table. Okay, deal?**

That's a deal Angela, Yvette responded with a thumbs up. That's a much welcomed homework assignment, Yvette laughed. I can't wait to get on a massage table!

Chapter 11

What would I do If I could suddenly feel
And to know once again
That what I feel is real?
I could cry
I could smile
I might lay back for a while
Oh, tell me what
What would I do if I could feel
        - What Would I Do If I Could Feel, The Wiz,
        Charles Emanuel Smalls.

Six months after my first Essence Festival experience, I met my next baby's daddy.

I was high off the rush from my new lease on life, so I let a girlfriend convince me that I'd be just perfect for her Godfather. She introduced us and we hit it off right away. His name is Dre' and he is ten years my senior, lives in Detroit, is college educated, had no kids, and was worked as an Accountant for a major car manufacturer. He told me that he was ready to finally leave eligible bachelorhood and settle down with a family. He claimed that he also had a new lease on life after having recently attended the Million Man March, which had an effect on him much like my Essence Festival experience did on me.

Because I lived in Atlanta, we spent most of our days talking over the phone. In fact, we called each other every day for six months, often two or three times a day! We had great energy and couldn't go a day without hearing each other's voice. Eventually, I flew out to Detroit to spend his birthday weekend with him. He was celebrating his 37th birthday. We had incredible chemistry. We laughed so much and genuinely enjoyed each other's company, not to mention he was easily whipped when it came to having sex with me!

Within a week of my return, post-rendezvous, he was practically begging me to move to Detroit and be with him. Dre' was adamant that he wanted to be with me and that I was *the one* for him. So yeah I fell for it and silly me, I quit my job, moved out of my condo and headed to Detroit with my son, on a whim, a wing, and a prayer. Initially, I lived with my girlfriend who I had lived with before back in high school – because I didn't feel comfortable moving in with Dre' right away, especially with my son. Moni was now also a single mom with a son around Junior's age, so she and I were roomies again, at least until I got to know Dre' better. Dre' really wanted me to move in with him, but he settled for me staying nights until I got comfortable with making things more permanent.

Well, things were great between us for about two months. Then, one night at his house, we were asleep in bed and a crazed woman started beating on his door and accusing him of cheating on her. She slashed his car tires and cursed him out, until the cops came. Needless to say, that was the end of he and I- and the beginning of my morning sickness. Yep, I was pregnant. And Dre' wanted me to have an abortion, because I wasn't coming back to be with him. But he was a liar and, she was right, he was a cheater. As I'd come to find out, he had been in a relationship with that woman for years.

I was done with having abortions and Dre' knew this because we had deep discussions early on in our relationship about it. A large part of my "new lease on life" was that I was ready to grow up and be accountable for my own actions. Plus, I had promised God that my last abortion was the last time for me, and especially after suffering through the ectopic pregnancy a year ago. (Deep down inside, I felt that was punishment for having abortions.) So Dre' knew how I felt, and knew that I felt near and dear to my new found principles. We had in-depth discussions about my beliefs during those many lengthy, daily phone calls before I came to Detroit; so with or without his help, I was going to have this baby.

He let me know flat out that if I didn't want to be with him, then he wasn't going to help me with this child, so I ended up going through my pregnancy without his help. I moved back to my home town to be closer to my family while I pieced together a plan to bounce back from yet another bad relationship decision. I gave birth to a beautiful baby girl on June 19, 1998. I named her

Heaven-Imani, based on a dream I had while I was pregnant. In the dream, there appeared an image of an open bible with praying hands beneath it and the words 'Always having faith in H.I.M.' and, I interpreted the acronym as her initials, Heaven Imani Morgan, which hence became my daughter's name. I often remind her that Heaven is where she came from, Imani is because I will always have everlasting faith in her and, *Morgan* represents the fact that she will always be daddy's little girl until her soul mate comes along, even if it didn't seem like it.

So, the lesson just keeps showing up for you; you are going through relationships with what sounds like 'love goggles' on and you can't see what you're really working with because of your desire for a fairy tale ending, right down to the naming of your daughter. You've started talking about making changes and yet drama still continues to show up. The difference is that I hear the optimism in your voice now.

Well, for the next seven years, it would become my ritual to return to the Essence Festival and participate in the seminars. The Essences Festival was my revival, y'know, like the ones Christians attend? It's like in this annual event, I found *my* church! I found *my* gospel and it allowed me to keep my head above water and focus on what was important to me. I finally found a way to get out of my own way, and I applied this to my daily life while I watched my life change in some aspect every day! I became consumed by the surrounding positivity and hope possessed by the other attendees at this empowerment conference. I wanted the kind of transformation that the guest speakers said they had! I was so empowered by the positive, triumphant stories that could bring a smile to the most pessimistic face. I envisioned me up there on that stage one day sharing my story of personal triumph and transformation and how my life was elevated. I had a new way of thinking and being, despite my past decisions and circumstances; I knew a better me was possible.

I see now that you have been on this journey and will remain on it because you continue to discover more about yourself and want to continue that. Coming to see me is about processing that while you keep

**learning more about yourself. I want to go back to the
time you spent being proud of your body and using
it to get both attention and money. Do you feel any
connection to what happened to you when you were
eleven? Then at seventeen? And again at twenty-one?
Does a theme about self-worth or value come up for
you?**

I would have to think about whether I was actually proud of
using my body for money or attention once I was aware of the
connection from the past sexual violation and exploitation. As it
stands, the answer is, *no,* I don't see the theme and or connection
as a whole, but there have been times when I felt proud that I
was fine as hell and could use that gift to my advantage. So, yeah,
maybe there is definitely a theme there.

Let's see, Yvette said with an attitude…the theme might just be
that at age eleven I was violated by a man against my will! This,
of course made me feel less than, and unworthy! That, coupled
with the messages beaten into my head over and over in church
and in my Catholic school that God favors girls who are virgins,
girls who respect themselves enough to wait for a mate to choose
them, because they are whole and pure and virtuous. Well
that also made me feel worthless because I knew that I wasn't
a virgin. So that meant that I would never be whole and pure,
therefore never feeling "virtuous"! And the final blow came from
the lyrics of that damn song *Dear Yvette.* With lyrics that made
me ultimately feel that I was certainly not good enough! Here you
have the most famous rapper of all time saying that I wasn't!!!

I really hate that song, Yvette exclaimed. That song, the
pervasive theme of not being good, pure or wholesome enough had
replayed itself over and over in my mind like a badly scratched
record or like fingernails on a damn chalkboard! These repeated
messages had ingrained themselves so deeply that I became the
three things which trouble me the most: less than, unworthy and,
not good enough.

**Ok. So then let's reflect on that theme of being less
than and unworthy a little bit more! Can you tell
me why you think you kept getting pregnant? I want**

to understand if you continued to have unprotected sex because you felt like you didn't need to or was it something else?

Yvette pauses for several moments before saying, "Pleasure factor, I guess. Hell, not really though, because I honestly didn't "make a" decision about having unprotected sex! I mean it's just what I'd always done. When my uncle started having sex with me there was not "protection". I eventually became aware of STD's and pregnancy but, I never thought about being preventive.

Wow! Now that I actually say it out loud, it sounds crazy! I can only assume that maybe I was operating with a *pleasure first* mentality. I truly wanted better for myself, but it was easier to execute this desire in my head more than in real life. Having unprotected sex is what I'd always known and done, just as I had abortions to undo what unprotected sex did. I realize that, for twenty years, I operated from a place of familiarity. I worked from a familiar script, directed by the looping metadata in the recesses of my subconscious. It had been said that this is how we, the less than, the unworthy, and the not good enough girls, do it. For that long quest for the fairytale love, the love I always desired from my father but didn't feel like I received. I embraced the attention-however meager and superficial- that I was able to garner from other men the way Uncle Alonzo taught me to. I know I was on a chase to fill that void. I am not a bad person though and I didn't deserve to be treated like one or stereotyped as one or described as such, the way that I felt like I was in *Dear Yvette!* Yvette yelled as she started to cry out loud.

That's good Yvette, Angela says as she places her hand on Yvette's back. Sit up for me and breathe Yvette. Allow yourself to feel that, Angela says as Yvette begins to bawl. The two of them just sit in Yvette's cry for several minutes. Then Angela continues...

The pregnancies, including the ectopic one, go back to second chakra imbalances, but because your adult heart is involved it is also involving the fourth chakra. I want you to do the following affirmations right now. Here, hold this mirror. Look at yourself and repeat

the following:

Today I choose to take the limits off of my love. I am the love of my life.

Today I choose to take the limits off of my love. I am the love of my life.

I love in a way that brings order and harmony into my life.

I love in a way that brings order and harmony into my life.

I take complete ownership for the state of my life.

I take complete ownership for the state of my life.

As I begin to love and accept myself, healing occurs naturally.

As I begin to love and accept myself, healing occurs naturally.

I am strengthened each time I make the choice to love myself and honor my body.

I am strengthened each time I make the choice to love myself and honor my body.

Angela then hands Yvette a paper with the affirmations along with some additional information on it and says...

Keep these affirmations in mind, Yvette, as you go forward through the week until our next session. The other thing that I want you to do is to think of a song. A song that helps you to define your state of mind knowing that you have to love yourself before anyone else can reflect what you see in the mirror.

Today I choose to take the limits off of my love. I am the love of my life.

I love in a way that brings order and harmony into my life.

I take complete ownership for the state of my life.

As I begin to love and accept myself, healing occurs naturally.

I am strengthened each time I make the choice to love myself and honor my body.

What are the songs in the key of life for you? Love, success, marriage, children? What will make life perfect for you? We can chase our idea of what is perfect and when it is within our hands, we sometimes realize it was never our idea in the first place. If we take the time to think about what truly makes us feel joy, it is rarely tied to a dollar sign or a material possession. When we are moving in our true purpose and swimming in the seas of our own divinity, we do not have to contort ourselves into cumbersome positions to fit into our own lives. You will never have to force and manipulate anything or anyone into your world; what belongs to you is already yours. What is divinely yours will flow through your life as effortlessly as the waves do the sea.

Thanks to science, there is a substitute for almost everything we eat, drink or wear. However, what truly sustains us—faith, hope and love—have no equal. A life well lived cannot exist without these three. When we are young, we play at being-being a doctor, being a teacher, being a musician-and there is nothing tied to the action other than the feeling of happiness we derive from it. Think about what makes you happy and it will likely lead you to something of which you are not the benefactor-the joy is in the giving. We

spend a lot of our lives searching for the three necessary supplements given to us at birth and reinforced daily— they are already yours. Once your heart is open to the recognition that you possess what you need, that is when your mind makes the connection so you no longer seek to find that which is already yours.

Chapter 12

You know that you want more
What are you waiting for
I think your ready now
Forget what they told you
World can't hold you now....
- *NOW by Ayanna Gregory*

Were you able to come up with a song? Angela asked.

Yes! And I even have it on my phone. In honor of my favorite hip hop artist of all time! R.I.P. Heavy D, my biggest fairy tale prince! I'm even going to sing it for you on the microphone!" Yvette smiles wide and belts out: *Now that we found LOVE what are we gonna DO with i-i-i-i-it? Now that we found LOVE what are we gonna DO with i-i-i-i-it?"*

That's an excellent question. I hear that song and it makes me happy too. I've never really paid attention to the lyrics though. Yvette interrupted laughing...

No. Even though I love my Heavy D, I'm actually not sure about the lyrics to that song either, I just love that part of the song. It makes me feel good! Yvette said. But I was being silly, that's not the song that I chose. I actually chose a song that I heard recently and it brought me tears to my eyes and dang near brought me to my knees because the lyrics pierced my soul. I listened to all of the lyrics of this song and know that they are true for me! It's a song called "Now" by Dick Gregory's daughter, Ayanna Gregory, who is an awesome indie recording artists. Here let me play you a little bit of the song via my phone:

Always played the victim role
To satisfy my need to be right
Always feeling so alone
Neglected by the men in my life
But they was just doing what I wanted
See they was just giving what I gave
But now I want the real thang
So let it be a new path I pave...

Afraid of my destiny
Who I am to live to be
The Universe keeps blessing me
Every single time I renege
Filled with insecurities
Sabotaging royalty
Planned mediocrity
Self-fulfilled prophecy
Afraid to let them see
Who is she....
I know that I want more
What am I waiting for
I think I'm ready now
Forget what they told me world can't hold me!

Wow Yvette... That's powerful!

Now that's what I want for you to hear when you start to doubt yourself!

I want to go back to the relationship you had built with your daughter's father, Dre', for a minute. You never said you were in love, but you did say he was whipped. At that point, you were still discovering just how powerful sex can be. Do you associate the drama between sex and love throughout your adult life with your perceived self-value? I ask because I haven't heard you say that you fell in love or felt loved any more, after Morris. You also haven't said what it is you truly desire.

By that time I was grown, sexy, independent and single but tired-I was oh so tired of the games played and the vast web of lies that plagued my life. I had grown so tired of the status quo I couldn't take another liar, nor another lie; not even my own. I had to give up ghosts and fairy tales. I had to begin to tell the truth, to be the truth, my own truth. I am a single mother of two beautiful children who I am both eternally grateful and solely responsible for. I must remain present for them in all things and at all times. Whether I like it or not, neither one of their fathers are present in their lives regularly and this I must accept, although I wanted so much more. Always, always I wanted more, I just didn't know more of *what* exactly, but I was gonna figure it out.

So I began to delve into my passion for music. That trip to see *The Wiz* with my mom ignited it so long ago. It sparked a passion in me that never died-no matter the places I've been or the things I've experienced along the way. I believe in the power of music and I felt the desire to bring the love back to music. I wanted to team up with the best of the best creative talents and aspiring artists, bring them together to create my very own Motown-like legacy. Greatness-we were going to create successful Grammy Awards-level greatness. This was my desire.

Fueled and focused, renewed passion, and a new vision in mind, I began to make moves to create *my* dream. I hooked up with a colleague who worked at Sony to get things started. We decided to create an Indie compilation cd that would make the world take notice of the talent that we represented. We called this cd, 'Club Midwest'. It was unmistakably created with much love and passion for good musical talent and we knew, if we did it right, that the world would precisely love this cd as well.

This project highlighted our artists' greatest talents and represented the diverse vibration of the urban sounds of the Midwest. I teamed up with an iconic female musician in Detroit and an amazing male producer from Atlanta to co-produce, mix and master this awesome project. All of my savings, all of my time, all of my energy, all of my resources-my whole heart went into this project, because I believe that you gotta be all in if you're going to win.

Everything that could have happened to make each piece of this dream come true was happening. I met the right people at the right time, said the right things in the right places, and made the right agreements with the right connections, and it all led to things falling into what *I believed* was divine order. My partner and I met some industry heavy-hitters who helped birth our creative baby. And we were so grateful for them because we were first-timers doing big things!

The ball was really rolling now and we were all smiles. We turned all of our music catalog over to our new partners. *Club Midwest* was in the final stages of mixing and mastering. It felt so good to be here, to see a piece of my dream come to fruition. It was a beautiful feeling. And just as I was enjoying this peace cloud, it evaporated. Suddenly, the phone calls started going to voicemail with no return calls and no one knew where the Club Midwest music files were- not even the engineers. No-fucking-body knew nothing about anything anymore! We had been played... It was some old gangsta' hood shit-the fucking story of my life! I just couldn't seem to have a happily ever after with any damn thing! The whereabouts of months of hard work, dedication, dreams and commitment resulting in nothing but a few whispers as to what might have happened. I sacrificed it all and lost it all. Eventually, I got an unexpected call from one of the assistant engineers on the project. He informed me that the catalog was stolen right from under us and that others were profiting from it. It turned out that we would never receive a dime from that project!

The assistant engineer and I brainstormed for a couple of months trying to figure a way to get our music back. But I was surprisingly contacted by his wife, out of the blue. She told me that he had died. The only person I could trust in light of all that was going on, and a friend, had been taken by a heart attack! Damn, he was young too. Only in his early 30's! Then shortly after his death, I'd hear of the loss of Left Eye, a well-known, well-loved member of that inner circle. What? I'm crushed-so much death. Death becomes a persistent, very real, very strong part of my life. Around this time, people that I knew were dropping like flies and I felt like my belief, my faith was being tested. I question *what happened to hard work reaping great rewards?* Apparently this is just another shattered fairytale, something else to snap me back to my harsh reality."

In 2000, I had flown to LA to attend the Source Music Awards and during a brief layover in Phoenix, I looked across the lobby and noticed an interesting man who was also waiting for the connecting flight. Our eyes locked for a moment and I remembered feeling an attraction to him, but I just kept it moving. We both boarded the flight and when it touched down in LA, I headed over to the baggage claim to meet my friend, who was a music producer, and his manager. They had also just arrived at LAX. We were all there to attend the awards show together. So after we all met up briefly, they left to get their bags and I waited for my luggage. As I waited, I felt this strong sensation that I was being watched, and I was! The guy from the Phoenix airport was there in the baggage claim area and he was staring at me!

He eventually made his way over next to me, staring the whole way so I sarcastically said, 'Take a picture, it'll last longer.'" He apologized and offered his hand to introduce himself. I shook his hand, told him my name then left to go meet up with my friends again. We all stepped outside of the busy airport to hail a cab and of course, I ran into the Phoenix guy again. Only this time, instead of talking to me, he was joking around with my friends! Upon realizing that they all knew each other, the guy offers me his business card and invites me to dinner. I was totally disinterested but cordial, so I took the card and he gets in a taxi. As his taxi departs, I shake my head, thinking, *whatever dude*, but my friends begin to rave about how I better call that man because he is rich and he is big-time in the industry. So now I'm thinking Bingo! I may have hit the jackpot here.

My friends encouraged me to call him and so I did and later that evening he and I went to dinner, totally missing the awards show. I learned that he's a young industry mogul and a self-professed member of the Billionaire Boys club and he appears to have this low key gangster mentality. Very intelligent, and quite charming, he said that he brokered multi-million dollar deals, wrote successful business plans, and funded businesses in the entertainment industry. He wasn't drop-dead gorgeous, but he's my type of fine-y'know that nerdy, yet distinguished looking kind of fine.

We started communicating regularly, talking on the phone every day, but with our busy schedules, we only physically saw each other two or three times a year. The low frequency did nothing to quell the intense magic, though. I'd never been so swept off my feet before, and I fell in love with him-hard. I was just gaga over this man, he was my Mr. Everything! He became really supportive. He wanted to help me pursue my dreams and offered to help get some of my artists signed to record deals. It sounded so good, but my freakin' pride got in the damn way. I didn't want him thinking that I was only after his money or connections. So I worked hard at keeping my time with him strictly about us and not the industry.

Then I made a big mistake. I introduced him to some of my music colleagues and *they* wanted access to his connections. He set up a few situations for them and unfortunately, one of these deals went bad. To this day, I still don't have the full story on the ins and outs of it. But one of my colleagues accused Mr. Everything of stealing $2,500 and a very talented, unsigned artist from right under our nose. She said that he took the young artist to New York City, signed him to a major label, all unbeknownst to me and with zero credit to us. Even now, my colleague accuses me of knowing something about the situation, although I didn't.

Through all of this, I approached Mr. Everything about my previously stolen project, he told me to get over it because I'd never see that music again and there was zero recourse for me to take. He also told me that he knew of the project and had knowledge it was used to secure a multi-million dollar deal for a well- known music producer in the industry. He insisted that I just needed to chuck that up as a loss. Just like that-no support! Unbelievable, right? But, he was just "keeping it real" with me, let him tell it. I accepted the *"real"* because I still found him charming and we just continued to get really close. At least, that's what I thought, anyway. We continued to talk several times a day over the phone. He confided in me. We were dating for about eighteen months and even talking marriage and children.

In hindsight, I see how he became my escape from the heartache surrounding *Club Midwest*. I regret not allowing him to help me with that when he wanted to. (I am much more open to receiving guidance now.) We were well into our second year together when one day he called me from the back seat of a taxi, bawling, complaining of being in excruciating pain and that he was losing his eyesight. He was on his way to an emergency room there in Atlanta, but I'm Michigan. So immediately I start making arrangements to get to him. But when I tried to let him know I was ready on my way to him, his phone kept going directly to voicemail. I'm a functional wreck at this point, wondering what the hell could be going on with him, so, I call the hospital where he told me he was heading to and I was learned that he was there in intensive care. It wasn't until hours later that he was placed in a room and I was able to place a call directly to him.

Worried, afraid and in deep prayer, because I had no idea of his condition or what is going on with him; I felt truly helpless. Finally, my call is connected and a woman answers. Clueless, I say *hello* and, ask to speak to him. She responds by saying, 'This is Tracy, his wife. Is this Yvette?' I paused in shock. I thought "Wait a minute. What? Wife? I was done! Gone! Literally, checked out. Without much thought, I replied, 'Yes.' She inform me of his condition: "He's been diagnosed with an aggressively acute form of lupus…" I just couldn't go on, I was still stuck on "This is his wife Tracy." Everything beyond that was slurred, slow motion, drowned out by my shock. I couldn't cry, scream, or curse his black ass out-nothing. Later, I'd find out-via the wife-that they had been married for five years and they have a two-year old son.

He epitomized more of the same bullshit I had dealt with for so many years. Liar, liar pants on mutherfucking fire! I was just sick. I hated him for getting me caught up in this bullshit. The nerve of this negro! Man, me and men- this love thing, I guess we just don't mix. So many disappointments. He called -they always do- of course, leaving these half-dead sounding messages, apologizing and, trying to explain. Just more of the same-the cycle continues. I curled up-tightly in a ball-and dropped quietly out of the industry. Add Mr. Everything's lying and married to some-damn-body-else's ass to the growing list of things both dead and dead to me."

More death… You still haven't taken the time to process anything that has happened in your world, have you? Processing grief is never easy. There is no way around it. It takes time and I hear in your words that some of those transitions have really stayed with you over the years. Especially the grief you have around the music. Let's pick this up in the next session.

**For your self-guided work today, Yvette, I want you to
fill in the blank lines on this letter and then say these
affirmations three times daily until our next session.
Because we talked so much about losses to death, if
anything comes up before our next session, I want
you to feel free to give me call and if it sounds like we
need to have a special session, we can do that as well,
ok?**

Yes. Ok. I will call if something comes up that's too emotional.
Thanks Angela, Yvette responded as
she received the homework.

Dear Young _____,

I know you are afraid. I know you have been hurt. I understand your feelings of repeated heartbreak and loss. It is perfectly fine for you to feel the fullness of your hurt, considering your experiences of _____

_____

_____. *The only way to work through pain is to allow yourself to feel the fullness of it. I am here for you, I am here to comfort and protect you. I want you to know that love is never lost, love never dies, love transitions. Although what was is no longer, it has opened the door for you to experience love on greater level. Have gratitude for all of your experiences. Gratitude transforms broken hearts into open hearts. Your openness will allow you the space to move beyond the pain of the past. Your openness will clear a field of vision for you to see beyond the fears of the future. You will be opened to showing up as love, and allowing love to enter and spill forth, creating experiences of* _____

_____ *peace and joy.*

With Love,

_____,

AFFIRMATIONS

I am always safe and supported.

I freely give and receive love.
I am loveable.

In all situations, I choose love and healing. Today, I let go and let God.
I express infinite love and gratitude for the time shared with my loved ones.
Heartbreak is temporary, unforgiveness makes it permanent.
Love never hurts, judgment does.

_____

_____

_____

_____

_____

Chapter 13

I'll search low, and I'll search high
Tryin' to find myself a cutie pie
But destiny leads me to a dead end (love somebody)
Over and over and over again
They told me to wait, so I waited
Anticipated, debating' and delayed it
But still came up with the same ol' thing
– Somebody For Me, Heavy D

Well, it's now, 2002 and at this time, me and dating-we're not friends, at all. I had no time for it, so when a friend of mine, Gina, told me about her online dating experiences, I was like, 'Uh, yeah, whatever, no thank you.' But, she persisted. Every single time we talked, she pushed. Eventually I let her talk me into entertaining the idea of finding love on the Internet. While at a week-long church revival, I decided to leave my darkness behind, to pray and fast. I turned the TV off for a week and I drank a gallon of water a day, and read all the verses in the Bible about love, joy, faith, hope, and peace.

Well this was such a powerful, totally transforming time for me that I vowed to do again the following week. But the next week, I replaced the Bible verses with forgiving people I had hurt and those who'd hurt me, some of whom I contacted directly, both to apologize, and ask for forgiveness. For others, I wrote open letters in my journal and forgave them from within. This process led me to compile a double sided list on a sheet of paper. On the left side, I listed the positive traits I desired in a man, and on the right side, I listed the characteristics of men from my past that I did not desire to encounter again. I took this list of pros and cons, folded it in half with the pros facing upward, and placed it in my Bible.

> *Now only three remain; faith, hope, and love. But the greatest of these is love.*

So a couple of weeks later, I agreed to join Gina on one of the first internet dating sites designed for African Americans. I gave myself strict guidelines, foremost in importance was honesty. I had to be honest in order to attract honest so for the first time, I posted current pics. I was fully open and honest in my description of myself and everything else, for the first time ever. And since I'm being totally honest, let it be known, the man of my dreams has always been Dwight Myers, professionally known as the rapper Heavy D. I always felt love from Heavy D's music! So I normally buckle at the sight of a thick, light-skinned, glasses-wearing, sexy swag-having man, who- in some shape or form- reminds me of Heavy D.

Well, the first dude to respond to my profile called himself 'Heavy Me'. Ha! I was so excited when I received a message from him that Gina had to calm my ass down. He looked a lot like Heavy D, but a slimmer, cuter version. His name was Mark and he lived in Detroit; cute, educated and drove a nice car. Sagittarius and an engineer, by trade. He drove two hours to take me to dinner for our first date. We talked, we got to know each other a little better, and he seemed to be impressed with me, as I was with him. And, I was looking all kinds of cute that day. I was thinking this could be the start of something good.

So we started dating. He took me out a few weekends. First just me and then eventually the kids as well. We ultimately began double-dating with Gina and her dates. We were going strong for about three months when he finally admitted that things are complicated. He isn't married, he's separated but living at home with his mother. He waited three months to tell me he had been separated for *five years*. 'Why don't you just get a divorce? 'I asked him. His answer-although I can't recall the specifics now-was not convincing, so I cut him off. *Next*. Well, there were a few *Nexts* after encountering a few more Mr. Not- For-Me's.

So I decided I was good on Internet dating. I took my profile page down. I was just giving up on that option. Then a couple of days later the strangest thing happened though. I received an email from a man who said he'd seen my profile page and was interested in getting to know me better. He asked me to respond if I was interested. My verbal response was *How in the Hell* could he have seen my page? I had taken it down already. This freaked me out so I immediately called Gina since she's the expert. I needed her to explain to me how this was happening. She said it took 24 hours to close an account, and she knew the guy who'd contacted me; she'd spoken with him before online. She said he was a nice guy, just not her type.

What? She thought I wanted her discarded choices, her leftovers? I definitely wasn't interested now. Not until he sent me a picture and a brief poem. I'm a sucker for poets; I'm a *Love Jones* kind of girl. So, I eventually responded. We talked via email for several weeks before moving to the phone. Then we talked on the phone every day for hours at a time, and when that just wasn't enough, he drove in-all the way from Chicago-to take me to lunch. The rest is history.

His name is Brian. He is tall, thick, light-skinned, with glasses. Y'know, the nerdy type I like. He has a PhD and a very conservative and considerate personality and demeanor. On our very first date, he shares his personal story with me on how he got to this point of dating online and he wants to know the *truth* about me and my story. I found this attractive and very freeing because this allowed for us to cut to the chase. Finally, I could tell my truth, and as Heavy D says, 'I want somebody to love me for me.' I could tell he was genuinely interested in seriously getting to know *me, and not just sexually.*

We'd go to the movies and dine out a lot. Brian was well-mannered, chivalrous, and respectful; he courted me. Y'know, I don't know if that had ever happened, if I had ever been courted. Wow. After a month, during my birthday, he took me to a beautiful bed and breakfast near a ski lodge. It was an absolutely gorgeous place with a fireplace and an indoor Jacuzzi. He treated me like a queen the whole weekend. We ate, we laughed, we truly enjoyed each other's company; as I came to learn more about him and his past I realized I really liked this man.

Something else he shared with me -he said that the next woman he slept with would be his wife. I was so flattered because there was absolutely no pressure to have sex. This was all so new to me. His next wife though? I thought; he'd been married three times over a period of thirty years, and he's ten years older than me. That's a big leap, and this is quite a bit to take in. So instead, I just enjoyed the rest of our weekend, thinking, *let's just see where this goes.* And it goes. It goes extremely well.

We began seeing each other several times a week, sometimes at his place and others at mine. We fell hard for each other and several months later we finally had sex and shortly after that moved in together. We were a ready-made family; his two girls fit perfectly within the nine-year gap between my son and daughter.

Junior was in middle school now and he was not at all happy about sharing his mom. There was an adjustment period, but he would eventually come around. After six months of this arrangement, of us being a family, we declared ourselves spiritually wed. So much about this felt right, so much about him was right, so much about us was right; our philosophies and attitudes were in sync and we were grounded, spiritually. Both of us opted against the confinements of engaging in organized religion, and we both have a strong love our people, black people. We love other people from all races as well but we were committed to being positive contributors in our community, we were committed to making a difference.

Brian insisted he pay all of our bills, and he took care of the hard stuff around the house. He was an excellent father, too. He was the answer to my dreams! He was a real knight in shining armor. Wow, there goes that fairytale shit showing up again.

For the first time, I allowed myself to be true to myself and fully show up comfortably as myself in this relationship. This led me to want to seek an even deeper level of truth about my authentic self.

Chapter 14

Believe in yourself, right from the start
You'll have brains
You'll have a heart
You'll have courage
To last your whole life through
If you believe in yourself
 — *If You Believe, Charles Smalls, The Wiz*

Around this time, I attended one of the best events I've ever experienced. It was a spiritual workshop in Maryland called *Wonder Woman Weekend*, facilitated by Iyanla Vanzant. This three-day retreat for women exceeded anything I could have ever conceived of in terms of self-healing. It's designed to support women in overcoming past issues while connecting with a deeper, more meaningful purpose in our lives. For the entire weekend, we released the darkness of our pasts and ushered in new, shining light, via our renewed, positive energy.

At this retreat, we were instructed to close our eyes and reach with our non-dominant hand into a basket as we silently prayed for what we needed to spiritually receive guidance. I selected the word *courage* as an attribute for that weekend. This would be the attribute that changed my life. I saw myself in a new light after experiencing courage on a richer, deeper level that weekend. That retreat blessed me with the courage to open myself up to making better choices that would elevate my life instead of destroying me.

When Brian picked me up from the airport, he was taken aback by how different and beautiful I appeared. He seemed totally amazed. He said I had a glow and my face seemed lighter -happier, than it did before I left for the weekend. While driving home, I thanked him for blessing me with the opportunity to attend this life altering workshop.

Once I got back home, the first spiritual practice I began was meditation. Life's funny. I had purchased a set of meditation tapes from Iyanla years ago and these are the ones I'd now pull out, and dust off. Only this time, I actually listened to them. And as a result, I started meditating every day, and it turned out to be a really good practice for me.

I was so excited about the workshop that I called my best friend, Janice, who is a holistic massage therapist, Reiki master, and massage instructor. I told her about my experiences and encouraged her to join me when I returned to Inner Visions. After our conversation, the weirdest thing happened - I started having dreams of returning, but not just as an attendee. In my dreams, I returned to this institution, joined the staff, and held a very prominent role there. A woman kept appearing in my dreams, and often leading me to replace someone. I tried so hard to stop having these dreams because they were freaking me out, but they wouldn't stop. I thought I was losing my mind!

I felt really discomforted by it all. I wasn't used to having such vivid dreams that had seemingly clear messages. I told Janice I felt like the dreams were really about her attending the institute, and that I'm only having them so that I can influence her. When she asked why I felt this way, I told her because the woman in my dreams is a massage therapist, Reiki master, uses flowers, makes oils, and creates scent products! I told her that I don't have the slightest clue about most of these things! Janice on the other hand did, but she said she just didn't have the money to attend that institute. So I asked her to just be open to it and don't worry about the financial part of it now, it'll come. I begged her "Please Janice, can you at least be open to attending the open house with me?" She said yes and we attended!

Apparently God had other plans for me because Janice didn't end up joining the institute with me. Brian did. After we joined Iyanla's institute together, Brian and I drove out to Rhinebeck, New York to attend a mandatory week-long sabbatical, an experience that would prove to be ten times more intense than the Wonder Woman weekend where I caught glimpses of my courage in action. While we were in New York, I embraced two new attributes that were assigned to me. *Surrender* and *Acceptance*. God really had me working my stuff out, and this was just the beginning. I felt child-like walking through the halls, open and wide-eyed, amazed and intrigued by every interaction and experience.

Midway through our week, I had a very powerful experience. We were going to participate in a sweat lodge which is a Native American ritual designed to purify and detox our being. I'd previously read about Iyanla's first sweat lodge experience in her book *Tapping the Power Within*, where she describes having a vision of snakes-or maybe it was worms- crawling all over her, so I was a bit hesitant. But focusing on my attributes led me to render my final decision to participate in the sweat lodge anyway. Courage, Surrender, Acceptance. That became my mantra and with these three attributes I moved forward through my hesitation and had my first sweat lodge experience in Rhinebeck with my husband and the Inner Visions family. Brian's presence also helped me feel safe and blessed as well. I was so grateful that he was there for me.

In preparation, we were clothed in white sheets and told to maintain silence-no talking for the entire day. As we entered the sweat lodge, I observed the architecture. It was quite interesting, a beautiful teepee- looking thing. And, as the experience began -devoid of linear time- I began to feel. I mean, for the first time in a long time, I actually began to really *feel*. I could feel my heart beating. I could feel my breath, every inhale and exhale. In the sweat lodge I felt a divine sense of connection to the earth as I sat on the cool dirt ground. Initially, I was placed in the back of the sweat lodge, but as some of the other women left the lodge, I continued to move up and I eventually made it up front next to the hot stones. I remember feeling even more elevated. The steam from the stones opened me up and I could feel the aroma from the herbs enter into my being. I felt cleansed. All of the prayers and chanting elevated my spirit.

At one point, I began to meditate on how good I felt and how elevated, how lifted I felt in spirit so that I could marinate in the gratitude of being cleansed as I released what I considered to be ancestral, generational patterns within me.

In my meditation, I saw myself consciously releasing the guilt from being so sexually involved with so many different men. I released the lack mentality of not having enough money or opportunities, and the poverty mindset. I released the pain from being molested as a child and I tearfully thanked my ancestors for supporting me with getting to the point in my life where I could release all these things that I felt were blocking my ability to excel in life. I felt so grateful for my ancestors in that sweat lodge! I felt so connected to my grandma Carolyn and my uncle Billy, grandpa Sonny and his mother, my great grandmother who helped him raise my mom before I was born. I thanked them all for their love and I forgave them all for the transgressions that I had judged as unloving as I accepted that they loved me and the rest of my family the best way they knew how.

For that, I loved, accepted and thanked them all. All four of them were ancestors now and all four had meant the world to me when they were here on Earth. Now they covered me, protected me even from my own misguided choices and mistakes, as well as from the rest of the mischief in the world and I felt that, because I was reminded of my divine connection to these ancestors. I could go forth with courage as I surrendered knowing that I was divinely guided and protected and I could accept the blessings in store for me. The experience was so rich and powerful, hours upon hours of sustained and timeless ecstasy. Can you just imagine? I loved it! I felt so empowered that I didn't want it to end.

I was cleansing and clearing-culling at the deepest level, levels only accessible by Spirit itself. Just amazing-I experienced true communion with the Divine. This is how heaven must feel, I thought. As the day drew to a close, exhausted, and silent, we were released back to our cabins. I left the sweat lodge feeling like I could create greatness in this world! I recall kissing my sweetheart, hugging him, showering, and trying to fall asleep. But as I lay in bed, I just couldn't shake the feeling. There was this feeling, like a peaceful melody playing within my soul, over and over. So I just gently rocked to it, back and forth, until I finally fell asleep.

On the last day of the sabbatical, I found myself beside two awesome sisters I'd made a great connection with them over the course of the week. I knew one of them from the Wonder Woman weekend that I'd previously attended. Her attribute then was *love*, and I have loved her since the moment I met her. I know, it sounds cliché right? Well it's true! I overheard Sister Love talking with the other woman, Liz. She was sharing about how her dreams led her to join the institute, and I was ecstatic. I thought - she's having the dreams too, just like me! And then I overheard Liz say that she was having them, too. This was too much for me. In my excitement, I just had to interject and share my story. I hoped it wasn't rude, to just blurt it out, but I had to.

"Sorry for interrupting", I said, "but I can't hold this in any longer. I've been having these *same* dreams! My dreams are centered on me joining the institute, but the weird part for me is there's a woman who keeps recurring in my dreams. She is a massage therapist who also does Reiki, uses flowers, makes oils, and creates scent products. I have no idea what this means, do either of you?" They embraced me with a big hug and assured me that I was in the right place. The conversation continued over breakfast, where they told me that I should share the dreams with Iyanla. I wasn't sure about that though. *Come on, they're just dreams, I don't know about all of that! Telling Iyanla about my dreams? That's way too much- over the top.*

Later the same day, Brian and I attended the last session of the sabbatical. It was a celebration to honor all of the great work we'd each done on ourselves for ourselves. During the celebration, the sister Liz from the conversation at breakfast, approaches me, grabs my hand, and tells me, 'I have someone who I want you to meet.' She walked me over to a table in the corner of the room. It was a sacred space, a shrine dedicated to Iyanla's daughter. Liz picks up the photo of off of the shrine and hands it to me, then says, 'Meet the woman in your dreams.'

I couldn't believe this was real, but the photo was *her*! It was the woman from my dreams! I lost it instantly! I was crying uncontrollably like a baby. I was so shocked, as the tears streamed down my face, I said to Liz, 'I don't know what this means, I'm not sure what's being asked of me. Why is she reaching out to me?' Liz hugged me tightly to console me, and whispered in my ear, 'Time will tell you what this all means, Love. Don't worry. Just know that you are being guided with love.' I thanked Liz, and then silently gave thanks to the woman in the photo, who definitely had been the woman in my dreams.

Chapter 15

The Beast miraculously changed into a handsome prince. He said, "I was under a curse all these years and could only be relieved when someone fell in love with me. I am now cured of the curse because you truly love me." And then, Beauty and the Beast were married and together they lived happily ever after.
  —Beauty and the Beast

I was filled with such strong sensations of gratitude and intense confusion at the same time. I had never felt like this before. I was a veritable potpourri of emotions and tears were the only constant-an endless stream of tears. I returned to the cabin and attempted to tell Brian of the day's events, but y'know, there were no words. As we drove away from the Institute, I looked back and sighed. I had released it all. I was empty, and ready to return to the world. I was returning clearer, more spiritually connected; a conscious, divinely guided woman with a great sense of purpose - to share love with others and move my life forward with the courage to create the rest of my life in the energy of love cradled with greatness. I was empowered to be great at loving and accepting myself more and sharing my love with compassion around others. I also felt truly forgiven.

On our drive to Philly, we heard bits and pieces of news about a hurricane, but not enough to piece together, or be concerned because we spent most of the return trip talking and reflecting on our experiences. I kept thinking about all of the praying and releasing we did at the sweat lodge, and how this happened around the same time as this hurricane. I thought—now that's deep -way too deep. I wondered if something spiritual happening in one place could potentially affect something not tangibly connected somewhere else? I reflected on this connectivity and it reminded me of the stories I'd heard about slaves who were overthrown from slave ships during slave passages from Africa . And the myths about how their souls-the slaves who didn't make it past the Bermuda Triangle-were rumored to stir up the waters and ignite hurricanes from there. It got me to thinking, what if calling up the ancestors and spiritual guides at the sweat lodge was connected to the stirring of waters in New Orleans? After which I laid back in my seat and rested for the remainder of the drive because I was obviously thinking too much.

When we arrived in Philly, we found out the extent of the damage and devastation of the hurricane we'd only heard bits and pieces of along the drive. It was Hurricane Katrina. The images of the city of New Orleans left me numb. I couldn't believe the level of devastation. My heart went out to all of the people pleading for help and my mind was blown at the death toll that just kept rising. The cries to reconnect with missing family members, all the pain and anguish that was happening in real time right here in the United States looked like footage from an under-served third-world country. I was in shock. I couldn't fully connect to all of the peril or engage it because my spirit was still floating high above human reality. So I prayed silently and continued to commune with spirit, begging that help reach those in need throughout Louisiana and beyond because the entire world was affected by these images.

I prayed: *Help us through this, God. Cleanse and clear us all through this, God. Shift us ALL to a higher level of love and understanding, God. Guide us easily and effortlessly beyond this devastation, God. Save us all from the despair, dear God. Grant us the ability to be compassionate with one another as you Help us through this, God.*

I was amazed at how different the two worlds are; the spiritual world, at the lodge and the physical world, here, now. At the sweat lodge, there was a deep peace with a divine energy of serenity; but the physical world felt like a constant force-feeding of information, with a mix of chaos and confusion. It was so hard to return to this chaos and dysfunction again; it took me several days to readjust.

I dedicated my first year attending the Institute to learning, accepting, and healing myself. The heavy focus on Hurricane Katrina gave me a greater sense of compassion and gratitude for simply being alive at a time when so many lives were lost or turned upside down. I donated clothing, money, and offered up many prayers for divine support. As a result of being so plugged into the despair happening in the lives of others, I developed a heightened sense of gratitude for my own life and took my studies very seriously.

I sat in the front row of most classes totally engaged as I asked many questions. I was learning so much about myself. For instance, one of the things I learned that intrigued me was why I walked with my inner thighs rubbing together: this was attributed to my previous sexual abuse and how my body shifted to protect me. The body really is amazing! I also learned why I speak so loudly and passionately: this is because I'm determined to be heard by others now. I'm no longer ignored, the way I felt when I sought my mother's help from Alonzo.

I learned to identify my triggers, and lying is a big one; I can't stand a liar, and can sense one from a mile away. I know a lie when I hear one: that's because I was once a connoisseur of the trade. Additionally, I learned to identify the core issues that have raged throughout my life, which are fear of rejection, fear of abandonment, fear of betrayal and yes, fear of success! I learned these issues all stem from my childhood. Throughout my time at the Institute, I became a voyeur of my own life and gained near-orgasmic pleasure from unveiling the most deeply intimate details of myself.

One of my biggest patterns or cycles was getting into trouble with the law. For years I would find myself getting several traffic tickets, which lead to having my driver's license suspended. Once I even ended up in jail for a weekend. But I just couldn't understand why I kept finding myself in this predicament – getting in trouble for speeding or having no insurance or having no registration. The same shit over and over and over again. What I couldn't understand was why I wasn't learning my lesson. I felt picked on by the law. But I learned how this pattern is divinely more symbolic of me breaking spiritual laws and violations of divine rules and not personal at all as it relates to my relationship with actual law enforcement. Meaning that, the police were not just picking on me personally. Instead, it is personal to my relationship with my own inner spiritual enforcement. I had to learn to align myself with following the rules that I know are right from the inside of my being. I was just being so defiant and breaking all kinds of spiritual and moral rules!

When I opened up, I also realized that hustling was an unveiling characteristic that put me in a survival state of being and this made me unable to fully enjoy a better life. I'd have to drop the hustling mentality in order to truly experience an abundance of greatness. I would have to learn to surrender to the divine belief that my desires are already blessed. Already a *done deal*! So I don't have to hustle no more. I simply have to have faith and believe! This was huge for me, because I'd been hustling, grinding, and being hustled my entire life and I'd reaped the rewards: men, houses, cars, bad credit, several pregnancies, and several brushes with death. Damn, now that I think about it, hustling hustled me and that's why I ain't got shit to show for what I did all that hustling for after all those years!

As I dove deeper and looked at the true pain in my life, I saw the little girl inside me. She was abandoned by my dad, neglected by mom, and raped by my uncle. She was left unprotected and frightened, and she was rightfully insecure. It was from this pattern that I concluded that a life as an intelligent hustler was not the way to go. Even though I thought it was my way out, and a way to protect myself from the cold hearted, physical world. Until I learned the world was not so cold. My *choices* were cold. My *perspective* was cold. But just like the sweat lodge was warm, I learned the world could be warm, and loving, nurturing and fulfilling- how? I simply had to change my choices, change my perspective, and break through those harmful hustling patterns.

I spent the next eighteen months at the Institute changing my choices and perspective. As it turned out, the truth-much like the answer-was simple. If I was to have more, of what I desire, I would have to *become* more, so I did. I *became* more and more. I dedicated the next seven years of my life to self-exploration and discovery, more trusting, more loving, more surrender and becoming the real me, no longer chasing fairytales.

I spent the better half of 2006 focused- very intently, I might add- on completing the first year of studies at the Institute and planning my wedding. Yes, I said, *my wedding*. It's the thing I dreamed about as a child, but oh, when I actually say it - *wedding*. Yes! Y'know, it wasn't really about Brian and me necessarily-we felt no push to do things "right in the eyes of God". We were content with our spiritual union, our home, and our children, but our families and friends consistently pressured us to, well, do the *right thing.*

Brian had been married three times previously, but he'd never had an actual wedding, so I wanted to give him one. One he'd always remember. Besides, I wanted something that set me apart from his previous wives. Ah, there was that thirst for adoration creeping up on me again. I just wanted to feel like he adored me the most because He was the *love* of my life and my *only* husband! In my heart, I couldn't imagine us not spending the rest of our lives together. But every now and then, that negative chatter in the back of my mind whispered sour statements of unworthiness that lead me to think that maybe he wasn't as into me as I was into him. Deep down inside I was still feeling a little starved. I loved him and he loved me, but that just wasn't enough. I craved exclusivity; I needed to be *The One*. Doubt had made its way in – and sometimes good thoughts would turn into bad ones. I wondered-is he a serial husband? Is he really a good man? Would he marry again if we didn't work out? And sometimes, though, not too much, I felt like I wasn't really the one he'd been waiting for. These thoughts were very hard to swallow because the truth is that outside of my own insecurities he was actually an awesome man. He's a great lover, friend, husband, provider, protector, and father. So I knew I had to do some more work on my inner issues and myself.

The work of being fully present in our lives is never done. It takes a constant effort. I think that one thing people have to realize is that taking care of your emotional and mental health is the same as brushing your teeth; it's daily work, not something you can just read a book or attend a workshop and address your issues once and they are fixed. What tools did you pull out to handle that?

With my soul open, I returned my focus to our future plans. I did a lot of mediation. I also did a lot of praying. I did a lot of communicating my true feelings and desires. I learned to positively express myself in the moment verses suppress out of fear of how what I felt would be received. I did a lot of journaling and I utilized the support of my spiritual family from the Institute to process my stuff as well!

I came across the location for our wedding while researching local beachfront properties around my hometown. I stumbled across an article on lakefront properties that included an extensive history via a book called *The Black Eden*. I couldn't believe all of this history had taken place in a city called Idlewild just a couple of hours away from where I grew up.

When Brian and I took our first trip to Idlewild, aka *the Black Eden*, we both appreciated its rich, peaceful, rustic feel. Brian is an outdoorsy, country boy at heart, so he was in love with the place immediately. I, on the other hand, spend very little time outside in rustic places so I wasn't convinced it was going to work for a big wedding. Brian was so excited that he was ready and willing to teach me all sorts of new things about how to enjoy the divine primitive land we were on.

It was so much to take in all at once –marriage and *forever*. It's hard to imagine that after everything I've been through, everything I've seen and heard that I could actually be married forever. But, I told myself that-Brian loves me, just for me. This feels like the cycle has been broken, like a *real life* fairytale, like a dream coming true-for me. I'm in love, I'm in love, *I'm in love!*

We did our best to plan and execute our wedding in six months. And, for the most part, it all went over well without many problems. We made history on June 4th, 2006. We were married in an African-themed beachfront wedding at Idlewild. Ours was the first recorded African-themed wedding to ever take place at this location and the first one to take place beachside in many years; so we were the talk of the town. I know it's my wedding, which that makes me biased, but honestly it was breathtakingly beautiful. We had nearly 100 guests, among them both of my parents. Three, *three* generations from my mom's side of my family were represented in the wedding party. Both of Brian's parents were deceased and he is an only child, so my family became his family. It felt like one big high-energy, fun-filled family reunion. When I did finally have a moment to sit, and my eyes made their way down to my finger, I realized everything had changed. I am married- *married*.

It was beautiful, it was just like a fairy tale and I felt like an African princess. I don't know... I guess I hadn't thought about being fearful of a *shattered* fairytale. I was so caught up with the wedding. I felt pretty secure with him... What is interesting though is that- no sooner than we got married, and did everything *right in God's eyes*, all hell broke loose on the home front with my son. Literally.

The day before our honeymoon, I get a call from my son. He tells me that he's been stopped by the police, and immediately, my mind considers the worst-case scenario because I can hear the danger in his voice and the police in my hometown have a reputation of profiling black men. My own father was racially profiled back in 1999. He was falsely arrested and locked in a jail cell, kept naked for nine hours, during which time he was taunted and treated like he was in Abu Ghraib or somewhere. So when I receive this call from my son, I immediately realize the urgency, as my son recounts the situation: "These crooked-ass cops are trying to arrest me for telling them that they can't take my cell phone out of my car". This is what he tells me before he abruptly ends the call. Oh, we have a problem! A real problem, I think. And I, the natural-born problem-solver get right to work. I try to call him back to get his location, but there's no answer. Shortly thereafter a cousin who happened to witness the arrest from his bicycle called. After he gives me the location, I call Brian and arrange to pick him up so we can go together to get my son from the police station. Junior is already in custody by the time we arrive.

We rush over to the police headquarters and demand to see my son. We're able to speak with one of the arresting officers as he's booking him in and here my courage attribute kicks in. I employ my inner skills, and ask what him what exactly did my son do wrong. I listen intuitively as the officer replies. I look him dead in the eyes as he responds, observe his body language and spot a *lie*! I know this man is *not* telling the truth.

First, he says they stopped my son because his music was too loud. Then he says they arrested him because they found loose tobacco on the passenger seat, which led them to believe he'd just rolled a blunt and therefore had drugs in the car. Shocked by that accusation, I remembered I had just looked in his car window-there wasn't any tobacco in the front seat of his car! I then asked the officer, 'So where is the tobacco?' He stuttered, looked down and around nervously and said, 'It's still in the car.' When I challenged him on it, he switched up and said it had been bagged as evidence. This man was definitely *not* telling the truth.

While we waited, Brian insisted that we file a report and that we should launch an investigation. Then my son's paternal grandfather arrived at the police station, and like clockwork, Junior was released about twenty minutes later. When he came out, he hugged Brian, and me then he exited the police station with his grandfather right beside him. The two of them broke down crying, they were so overcome with disappointment. It was like they wept with the grief of millions of black men who had been falsely arrested before. And that's when I knew that I had to do something about this! As the two continued to walk, it became clear that my son's spirit had been broken, as was his grandfather's. I peered over at Brian. He was tense, yet stoic; he was clearly trying to be strong for me. This made me feel the need to be strong and fight to protect the spirit of all three of them in that moment. Three generations of the "same old injustice" had to end here!

As I watched Junior hug his grandfather, tears streaming from both of their faces in a shared and familiar pain, I roared in my heart, 'This stops here!' And I wondered, how was I going to fight this system - a system where fair justice often doesn't exist. I also realize that on a more personal note, once again triggered, here I am in my own stuff also, fighting to be valued. So the tool I use in this moment is deep breath. Breathe Yvette. Just breathe, is what I tell myself.

Junior left to spend time with his grandfather and Brian and I returned home to finish packing. We drove back out to Idlewild the following morning. We were blessed to stay in at a waterfront home where we had several amenities to choose from to help ease our frustrations: paddle boats, pontoons, bike-riding or, swimming in the lake. There was also a host of great local restaurants serving locally grown, home-cooked foods. It was a heavenly destination designed to ground us in nature and away from the rest of the world.

Amidst it all, though-waves whooshing, the rich aroma of crabs soaked in garlic butter, and every fresh, restorative breeze from the lake-I felt internally numb. My mind's eye was focused on only one thing amidst all of this abundant beauty -my son.

I try to surrender to my emotions and relax my mind a little bit but the phone starts ringing. Several calls come in, one after another. My family calls. The Sergeant from Internal Affairs calls. Community leaders call. The local press calls and Brian is not happy about all of the distractions taking away from the peaceful honeymoon that he planned for us to enjoy together. Although he tries to appear to be understanding, it's clear that he's displeased with not having my full attention.

We were here to have our Yoruba ritual of tasting the elements because we weren't able to do it at our actual wedding ceremony like we had planned to. So we were here to honor our promises of love, for better or worse, for richer or poorer, in sickness and in health by participating in an African ritual. For Brian, this was the most important thing in the world because he was so connected to the power of spiritual rituals and to affirming our commitment to one another. Primarily because he was now on his 4th marriage, and he really wanted to make this one work.

The four elements are symbolic of our individual sacrifices, they make up the harmonious whole. I couldn't argue with the beauty and importance of the ritual, so despite where my head was, I surrendered. We arranged for the local sister who'd help us plan our wedding to meet us at the lake and facilitate the African ceremony for us because this woman had told us that she was actually a Yoruba Priestess. So we were honored to have her officiate our experience. And this kept my mind off of my son, for a short time, anyway.

As the ritual began, she recited the Yoruba tradition of the tasting of four elements:

Taste now the sour, *for surely every life of integrity admits to its share of times that are less than perfect. As you experience life's disappointments as well as successes, we offer our love and support, without measure and without limit. So let us taste the lemon and say we will.*

Taste now the bitter, *for surely every life of depth will know its moments of denial and rejection when you feel turned away by life. As you encounter times when bitterness might take hold of your hearts, we offer our guidance and wisdom without measure and without limit. So let us taste the vinegar and say we will.*

Taste now the hot, for surely there is spice and passion in every enduring relationship. As you find and express your hearts' deepest longings, we offer you our respect and encouragement without measure and without limit. So let us taste the cayenne and say we will.

Taste now the sweet, *for the abundance of life which has brought these two lovers here to be joined in marriage will continue to pour itself out for their enjoyment. As you know the sweetness of married life in all its ages and stages, we offer our congratulations and benedictions without measure and without limit. So let us taste the honey and say we will.*

As we spoke these intimate vows to one another and embraced, it occurred to me that we'd just shared this moment with the priestess. This didn't sit too well with me either. I got this eerie gut feeling, as she tasted the flavors right behind us... Why is she incorporating herself into *our* ritual? After she left, I mentioned my discomfort to Brian and he said, 'It doesn't mean anything, you shouldn't overreact.' So, I didn't.

Shortly thereafter, I started to feel ill, so I returned back to where we were staying so that I could take a nap. Once I laid down, the phone rang, I smiled, noticing the caller ID; it was one of my good friends Cheryl. Cheryl is an established OB-GYN who is very rooted in African culture and traditions. She was also participated in our wedding ceremony. So I shared my feelings of discomfort regarding our Yoruba ceremony and she shared what many members of my wedding party had already expressed concern about that woman at the wedding ceremony. Apparently, many people felt that the Priestess was trying to sabotage my wedding. Cheryl laughed and brushed their whispers off as just rumors and they didn't tell me because no one wanted me to be upset on my wedding day over some assumptions. We, well, *she* joked about it, but something stirred up inside of me.

Chapter 16

"Yes, yes," said the Beast, "my heart is good, but still I am a monster."

"Among mankind," says Beauty, "there are many that deserve that name more than you, and I prefer you, just as you are, to those, who, under a human form, hide a treacherous, corrupt, and ungrateful heart."

– Beauty and the Beast

My second year at the Institute was extremely intense. This was the year that my goals, dreams, and desires would become focused and manifest themselves in ways that would move me forward. The Institute held us to a higher level of integrity this year because we were expected to now apply the principles we learned the first year.

I'm still engrossed in the battle for my son, which eventually became criminal charges for violating a noise ordinance. I still can't believe it, but that's what the city stuck on him. I researched, pleaded and prayed for strong legal representation and God delivered - again. My mother and I are also very close during these times. Our personal relationship has grown tremendously over the years. I have come to admire her personal strength & how she has completely turned her life around. She really has become my shero, and is my biggest fan and personal cheerleader! She is continuously inspiring me to follow my heart as I strive to do God's work in my life. So my mom came by my house one day out of the blue and shared with me a word that she said God told her to bring me from the Bible. It was Ezekiel 37. She shared with me the story of breathing life into dry bones. My passion to pursue justice for my son instantly now resonated as a divine task for me to also inspire others to advocate for themselves and the ones they love as well.

Without a dime to retain a lawyer, I prayed and meditated on receiving the support I needed to win this case. Soon after, I was blessed to hire some of the best civil rights attorneys in the state to represent my son's case, which generated quite a lot of media attention. I led massive civil rights rallies, marches, boycotts, sit-ins, and other peaceful protests. However, the time I dedicated to fighting injustice began to cut into my studies at the Institute. It would soon become clear that I'd need to make a choice between my son's case and my spiritual training, and so I did. I chose to pour all of my focus into winning my son's case!

Once I informed my husband of my decision, which was to put my training on hold, he insisted that I finish my studies and pointed out that he felt I was returning to my old pattern of quitting when things become too tough. To a degree, I thought for a second that he may be right, but I still didn't listen because my son's future was at stake, so I wasn't quitting. I was protecting my son. The justice system had already killed my father's spirit years ago, and I wasn't about to let them continue to break my son's spirit too. This was going to stop right here. So, although, I didn't formally quit the Institute, I did pull out and I stopped attending classes, a decision that would unexpectedly cost me far more than I could have known then.

My husband continued to attend Inner Visions while I continued to fight for Junior. The things I saw along the way led me to fight against other injustices within the community, like real police brutality and the scarcity of black teachers in our school system. I had become a civil rights activist during this time and God sent a new mentor my way - Reverend Jerry McNeely. He was quite knowledgeable of the tactics and misdealing of our local justice system, having had his own share of problems when he'd tried to expose the local injustices years earlier. He was a great support and ally to our family and helped guide us through bad lawyers, police harassment, and obtaining therapeutic counseling for Junior. I believe he is a major part of the reason why we won both the criminal and civil cases.

At one point, it seemed like we wouldn't make it through this, but we did. There were times it seemed like the criminal justice system was trying every trick they had in their arsenal to *teach us a lesson* along with many other young brothers from the neighborhood.

During these times, my son would go in a single day from the happiness of receiving good SAT scores, to depression from receiving a letter regarding his court appearance for an arrest that never should have occurred. Things were really touch and go for a while, but Junior soon received his acceptance letter to Clark Atlanta University, and, although there were still court dates, this news gave him hope.

Eventually, divinely we won! We won the criminal case *with an all-white jury*! With the case behind us now, we shipped Junior to Atlanta right after he graduated from high school. During all this, things were falling apart at home. I learned from one of my former classmates that my husband had to repeat his second year at the Institute. Not only did he not tell me this himself first, once I asked him about it he never did tell me what went wrong or why. Brian didn't tell me much those days. He was still resentful that I chose to drop out of the Institute and there was also the issue of him running off into the woods with that Priestess every chance he got!

Brian and I became very distant. If he wasn't at the Institute, he was off to the woods of Idlewild staying with her. He said that he was just going to be with nature and clear his mind. But every month, really? And for days and then weeks at a time? I was growing sick of it, but arguing with him only widened the distance between us.

I wondered, *could I be projecting*? Is this me projecting my feelings of being overwhelmed and abandoned onto him, especially now with Junior gone and me being alone with my daughter? Am I repeating an old pattern?

Things continued to feel distant and tense. In the five years my husband and I had lived together, I hadn't seen him behave as strangely as he had those past few months. On one night in particular-I'll never forget-it was a dark night, and I'm a light sleeper - I awoke to some noises I heard from upstairs. I peer over- it's almost three in the morning, mind you- and my husband is not in the bed. I can hear walking overhead, near my daughter's bedroom. I thought to myself, "that's weird, why would he be up there? This is unusual, but then again, *he's* been unusual."

So all kinds of negative thoughts take hold- I toss and turn and pray, *Lord please- I swear, if he touches my daughter, I'm going to...Lord please, don't make me kill this man.* I'm reflecting on all the unusual behaviors, they're all playing in my mind. I continue to pray for clarity, for guidance. Doubt sets in- Am I acting out my own fears of being molested as a child? Can I trust my own judgment? Did I marry a man who is capable of sexually abusing my daughter? My body is still, paralyzed, as my mind struggles to make sense of it all, wrestling aggressively with fear, doubt, and negativity. As images of my own worst fears flash through my mind, I tuck my head under the pillows, afraid of what I might see. I know I can't take much more of this. But, I battle with it some more. Wondering, worrying, reflecting. I just don't know. Fearing the worst, but not knowing what to do, I surrender. I surrender my will to God and he responds to me with a memory.

As I lay there in motionless fear, God takes me back mentally to 2004. I'm at the Wonder Woman weekend with Iyanla. She'd just concluded the weekend with a powerful prayer and a powerful ritual that benefits breaking the cycle of sexual abuse while protecting our daughters and future daughters of our daughters from sexual abuse. I believed in my heart, after that experience, that my daughter was safe, regardless of what any potential perpetrator had in mind.

So I wasn't about to let the creaking wood above my head rewrite that story. I applied the belief that my thoughts are powerful, and I chose a powerful thought - that despite my negative chatter, my daughter is divinely okay!

Seconds after I declared that GOD kept her safe, Brian returned to our bedroom, and, before I could even position my body to face his, I screamed "What were you doing upstairs, near my daughter's bedroom?" And before he could answer, I, now facing him, cringed in disbelief. There he was, naked except for a towel wrapped around his waist. 'You went upstairs like that?' I yelled. And he responded: "Yes I went upstairs like this, I took a shower, that's all."

But I just didn't get it. We have a Jacuzzi with not one but two-his and her- shower heads right here in our bathroom, and another bathroom, just down the hall, which also had a shower he could've used. "Why in the hell would you take a shower upstairs and walk around like that with all of these other bathrooms down here?' I continued, now with my hands balled up in fists at my sides. That's the most hurtful thing a man can be accused of, I know. So I held my tone and demeanor together to keep from exploding on his ass as he gave me his excuse, then I let him have it about the overall discomfort I'd been feeling lately regarding his *unusual* behavior-all of it.

"Why are you gone all the damn time? Look at how distant you've become over the last six months, right around the time I left the Institute. 'What did I do wrong?" I cried.

"I was upstairs praying over your daughter. I do this every night, I do this for all of our children", he said. And before I could apologize, he was so upset that he got dressed and left. I ran upstairs to check on my daughter, and she was sound asleep. I tried to wake her, but she barely woke and I decided to just let her go back to sleep. I went back down to my own bed, feeling horrible. I've never felt like this before, never sensed or accused anyone of hurting my daughter. This was such a strong and uncomfortable feeling, and I'm still not certain that it wasn't me projecting my stuff onto him. I felt horrible the whole night with just my own feelings of doubt to go on. I knew it was a horrible accusation, and I couldn't believe I accused him of such a thing, but he had been acting weird as hell! I just didn't know what to do or think, so I emailed Iyanla in the wee hours of the morning and shared my thoughts and the experience. And then I went to sleep, thank God.

The next day, I questioned my daughter intensely about her recollection of the night before, and she had no clue what I was talking about. She didn't remember anything and she definitely did not seem sexually harmed or abused in any way. I spoke to my husband about it again, this time apologetically, but I wasn't feeling his victim-driven response. He tried to make me feel bad for pointing out my concerns. This sparked another argument, and during the argument, I snapped!

Let's just say that I released tons of built up anger. I broke out five windows in our home. I just started throwing shit right through them. It was almost playing out in slow motion like I was outside of myself. All of this pinned up anger had overcome my sensibility. But, I actually felt a huge sense of relief after all of the yelling, screaming and throwing was done.

"You liar!' I screamed at the top of my lungs, "I can't take another one of your lies. No more secrets, no more lies, I am done!" And through it all, he didn't say a word, he just sat and watched in silence, like a deer caught in headlights.

And speaking of headlights, our neighbors called the police. When the police arrived, there was glass all over the place. As I looked around at all of the glass, I thought back to how my husband had wanted to make this very room his sacred space. We had been at odds over this particular room for over a year. I guess he could have it now, 'cause I was outta there.

It sounds as though you were so heavily involved in your son's case that anything that your husband was going through was being done alone. The broken windows reminds me of what happened with Alonzo. It seems like you get into what we call a dissociative state, meaning that your behaviors are other than what you normally display. Once your mind is set to something, it sounds as though there's no changing it. Did things start to get better?"

After this fiasco, it just got worse. Shut-off notices for our household utilities, frozen bank accounts, no food. Money is tight, my relationship is broken and another fairy tale has been shattered, just like all that glass all over the floor.

Brian left first. He rushed off to Idlewild again and was gone for several weeks this time, much longer than usual. I called and begged him to come back home, and when that didn't work, I begged the Priestess to send him home. She declined, stating "I am not going to do that because, he is always welcome in my home. And, know this, I love him just as much as you do." I

178

was completely blown away. Why should I be competing for my husband's affection, attention and adoration? And, get this, with a sixty-five-damn-year old woman. This is just unbelievable! At this point, I'm fucking done- I am done! Stick a fork in me- done. It was over.

By the time my ride came, I had a few suitcases packed with-a few essentials, but they couldn't fit along with all of us in the small sedan. So I dumped the suitcases out and took just the bare necessities with us in a garbage bag-one garbage bag. That's how done I was! Tired of all the chaos, the begging and pleading, tired of fighting for other people to value who I am. I was just ready to be loved again. Only this time, by me!

Yvette, thank you for continuing to freely share your story with me, because it helps me, help you. I'm going to suggest something that will help you to expel the psychological material that we have been working on and take your journey to a more transformative level. The first thing that I am going to refer you to do is some forgiveness work. In the form of a comprehensive combination of ancient Native American healing techniques and spiritual principles that will help you to accept everyone's role and responsibility in your life experiences. It is not to blame or judge anyone for anything, but allows you to forgive yourself and others involved, so that you can have a complete healing experience. The way that I'm going to have you do this is to have you attend a Radical Forgiveness Ceremony and then let you tell me about your experience. After which, I will send you to individually speak with the Forgiveness Life Coach, Kym Kennedy who will be facilitating the forgiveness ceremony. Your second experience with her will be a one on one coaching session and I will be video-conferenced into the session so that, if there are any major emotional releases from you during the session, I can assist with processing you through that.

Aside from the Radical Forgiveness process, I am also setting you up to see a spiritual energy healer named

Surayya who will support you through a second process called Metamorphosis. With this technique, Surayya will use Reiki to remove any energetic blockages detected in your energy centers that are connected to your previous traumatic experiences from conception throughout your present state of being. You will need to see this practitioner a few times. I will be video-conferenced into all of those sessions as well so that I can also continue to support you.

I won't be in the first session because that session is designed to formally get you two connected. But after that, we will be working together to support you. You can expect that these processes will be ongoing for you each week for the next 9 weeks.

Here is one last handout for you to read and I will see you back here in a couple of months!

METAMORPHOSIS-We all have our methods for coping, good, bad, effective and not. We each develop avenues to pacify our aches. Pain can push us to engage in self-soothing, numbing activities: promiscuity, drugs, alcohol, all of which may provide a temporary bandage that soon wears off, leaving the underlying torment to remain. Growth, and sometimes, emotional exhaustion, may lead to the development of techniques that offer better feelings, morning-after feelings, but these to, subside. But, with prayer, meditation, therapy, exercise, or friendships, we can develop the most positive system to assist us in our emotional survival. These provide longest-lasting, most deeply soothing results.

In lieu of tapping at the surface, we seek to exorcise our pain from its depths-the beginning. We learned, just as we are heir to our hair and eye color and other features, as are we heir to our emotional DNA. Unlike our genetic predispositions, we-intrinsic to all of us- have the power to stop inherited generational dysfunction. It takes courage to look beyond the surface and uncover all of the stuff we've been taught to hide- our fears, flaws and weaknesses. And once we dig up all of this muck, then what? Well, then, the road to true love and acceptance can be seen.

The road to true love and acceptance requires forgiveness of others, but most importantly, what is required is complete forgiveness of self. This isn't easy, and requires practice. But, it is one of the keys to your freedom. We know that we must learn to read, write and count, but when do we make time to study and honor the self? You are the subject, and only you can decide how, when or **if** you will move toward an environment that allows for love, acceptance and forgiveness.

Chapter 17

"Kill me," said the poor bird; and he bent his head down to the surface of the water, and awaited death. But what did he see in the clear stream below? His own image; no longer a dark, gray bird, ugly and disagreeable to look at, but a graceful and beautiful swan.

-The Ugly Duckling

9 weeks later, Yvette returns....

Welcome back Yvette. It's good to see you. You look great!

What did you think about the process?

That was so powerful Angela! Thank you for sending me to see those awesome women! I've done some forgiveness work before, so I really didn't think I needed it. But I was clearly wrong. That was incredible! Really! Even emotionally, I was amazed that I had so many things that I was still holding onto and fighting with within myself. And you were right, I just had to stay open and trust the process. Both of them were really good at helping me get to the truth about myself, which allowed for me to really forgive as I faced my divine truth!

First, Kym blew my mind with a lesson in the difference between *traditional* forgiveness and the process of *radical* forgiveness, which let me know that I probably hadn't fully forgiven anybody even though I thought I had. Then we went through all of the things that had ever been done to me and forgave those involved in the experience. And the crazy part was thanking them for the experience *and* forgiving them!

Now that you've done it, how do you feel?

I feel so much lighter. I've got a completely different perspective on my experiences. Now it makes sense why some of the best rape counselors were once rape victims or how some of the best drug counselors were once drug addicts or how some of the best cancer advocates are cancer survivors. It's almost like it's because, at some point, these people released themselves from the anger, fear, pain, shame and anguish of their circumstances and replaced that energy with the gratitude of being able to change their circumstances and their ability to make lemonade out of life's lemons.

This work helps you face the problems, feel the problems, and then free yourself from the problems, in a way that processes the negative energy you have been holding onto from your mind and body. The metamorphic technique operates on the premise that emotional traumatic experiences, from the moment of conception, can be held in the body and that by working on the reflex points similar to those in reflexology, that energy blockages can be released. I had talked in detail with you about your birth and life story. So I was comfortable that we psychologically processed you through it, but the energy connected to those thoughts and experience tend to stay in your body, so it's good that you were able to work with Surraya & Kym to shift it out of your soma!

Yes. It was good for me to experience that. I feel so relaxed and at peace now. I was really ready to heal. Fully and completely! I've never experienced anything like that in my life. Even though you told me, I did some research on it and I still didn't really know what I was getting myself into. But now what I know is that that experience was incredible! Surayya really went back to my conception and birth and was able to feel that chaos. She didn't even know anything about me, but she tapped right into it. That was amazing! Everything was literally in my feet and hands and head. It seemed like every time she tapped into my energy I was fine until she held onto it for a little bit longer until my emotional stuff was cleared. After she had held on to the point for, I don't know, maybe 15 or 20 seconds, I could feel that there was something there. It was like I was numb but then I could feel it. And then I could really feel it! I felt the energetic release of it all.

I couldn't believe when you said you could see that I was balling my fists up to prevent feeling that emotional release around feeling abandoned and how you had me take those deep breaths when I was holding my breath. I didn't know I had been doing it until we processed my 20s and that whole episode where I thought I was going to die. That time you were making me keep my eyes open when I kept trying to shut them when I was facing accepting that my mother and father really were there for me the best way that they knew how to be. You were telling me to make noises while I was breathing, because you said I looked like I needed to release. I still don't understand how you saw all of that through a video camera. How did you know what to do or say to me?

I've been working with the body and mind for a very long time Yvette. As I've said before everybody has a story. We just have to process the body sometimes to get to the core of the story, with love, in order to fully heal.

Once I got over my initial nervousness, things began to take shape wonderfully. I really had to own my truth about how angry I was and both of these practitioners created safe environments for me to relive these experiences. I felt comfortable enough to verbalize my truth. I was amazed that I had so many inner battles happening and I wanted to resist at first, but I let go and eventually began to trust the process. You were right, Angela, both of them were really good at helping me get to the truth about myself. This experience was a powerful nudge in the direction of uncovering my divine truth and healing myself. I know I said that I wanted to go back and do more radical forgiveness, but I don't think I need to do it now. What do you think?

Based on what I saw, your forgiveness sessions went very well for you. Your breakthroughs are evident in your presence, posture, walk, and talk. But there's still a little bit more work for you to do.

I accept that! Yvette smiled. During the process there, Kym asked me about the mental or emotional intensity surrounding my daughter's father, Dre. Initially I didn't think that there was anything there because I thought that I had been moved beyond any emotional upset surrounding him, but with Kym's coaching, it became evident that there was still some upset in me because, when we went a little deeper, I had a serious emotional breakthrough and was able to get rid of some remaining unforgiveness toward him. Three days later, and I literally mean three days later, I received a child support payment from Dre out of the blue, when I had not received child support from this man in over a year! And I am still consistently receiving them! So trust me, I now believe that the power of forgiveness cannot be underestimated. Forgiving definitely releases blockages surrounding my desires. So I am always ready to forgive now!

Are you ready to enjoy the rest of your best life? asks Angela.

Yes, but I have to say, I'm kind of wondering how much better can I feel because I feel pretty amazing right now! Yvette laughs.

I can tell when people are coming to the end of needing frequent counseling sessions because the breakthrough is evident in the way that they carry themselves. You, dear Yvette, are nearing the end and something will happen to or for you and it will be exactly what you need. It will be something that your subconscious mind has desired. That's when we'll know we've finished our work. When it happens, you will know it, and I will know it because you won't be able to help yourself from sharing. That's when we know we've made it to the other side. I will still encourage you to have a traditional therapist or hire a professional life coach to support your continued growth as you continue to evolve and manifest your desires. You can even come back and see me on an as-needed basis. Optimal mental health is just as good in prevention as it can be when things go wrong.

Understood. I really do feel pretty amazing. Thank you, Angela! Yvette reaches out to give Angela a hug.

You are certainly welcome, Yvette. I also want to encourage you to continue to use meditation, journal and use the affirmations. All of those things will help to keep you aligned.

I will. In fact, I have also begun to incorporate Chakra Yoga into my weekly regimen. It feels so good to be spending such intimate time working on myself. This is definitely a positive lifestyle change for me and I find myself not yearning for someone else to love me or admire me now that I am showing myself so much love and admiration. I speak to myself in the mirror in the morning and hug myself tight at the end of Chakra Yoga, all the while speaking the positive affirmations that you have given me. Eventually, I will embrace changing my eating habits to support the lifestyle changes that I am already making. But I am going to allow myself to take life one step at a time now, so that I can really enjoy it as I change it.

Y'know Angela, during this process I turned forty, and I celebrated it by hosting a Fire Walk.

What's a Fire Walk?

A Fire Walk is a Native American ritual where you walk barefoot across hot coals as a spiritual rite of passage, a test of an individual's strength and courage. As I walked across the coals, I knew the experience would direct me to the right path with regards to my marriage, my business, and my future as a whole. The event was so powerful and I enjoyed it so much that I returned later to walk across the coals again. It was clear to me that I came to win. I'm ready to win, and success is mine. I know it, I feel it, down in my core. I set the intention that I am successful in all of my endeavors and I affirm this daily!

Yvette's your awakening began with a visit to an empowerment conference. Upon hearing a seminar speaker audaciously suggest that you are worthy and valuable, both despite and in spite of your perceived transgressions, you felt moved- empowered to cast your doubts aside and pick up additional information

**and tools that, when paired with your natural
curiosity and thirst for knowledge, would lead you on
an evolutionary journey of self-discovery. I am really
proud of you butterfly!**

I brought with me a sheet of affirmations that I retrieved from a
newsletter from the Institute. I have been reciting them I desire
to share them with you. There are quite a few. They're not the
short ones that you had me doing either, but they mean a lot to
me. I have them taped on my bathroom wall. I also have a letter
that I wrote to myself in my journal recently. Can I read them to
you?

Absolutely Yvette. Let's hear them!

AFFIRMATIONS

I am fearless in my pursuit of love and wisdom.

I know that my greatest path lies within me and I willingly follow it wherever it leads.

I forgive myself for thinking that I am not perfect, not good enough, not smart enough and not lovable.

I claim my perfection, my enough-ness, my intelligence, knowing that I am loved and lovable.

I live in the present and envision my future knowing my Higher Power is at work in my life. In this now moment, I understand the true meaning of forgiveness.

To forgive others is to love and forgive myself.

As I forgive myself and others, I release anger and free myself to create a life that serves my family, my community and all of humanity.

I practice forgiveness and claim that the past has no effect on my present or future.

I no longer hold onto anger and resentment.

As I release negative feelings and destructive thoughts, I invite peace and harmony into my life.

I have the courage today to forgive my parents for any wrong that I thought they did to me.

I take responsibility for my anger, I take responsibility for any hateful thoughts and I take responsibility for destructive feelings.

I forgive myself for any grudges that I hold against my parents or those who raised me.

I am so grateful for the adventurous journey my life has taken thus far. I am glad to finally be at a place and in a space in my life where I truly trust myself again. I haven't been here since I was about 9 years old. I trust my decisions now and I believe that everything that has happened to me has truly been a divine assignment in the curriculum for my life's work and purpose. Now that I have intimately released all of the silently held secrets in my life, I can now release the judgments that created the drama and chaos surrounding them. I no longer embrace shame.

Spirit has led me to write a letter to myself from my own connection to my own learned lessons and I am so proud to be finally grounded in my own words, which represent my own truth. And the letter goes...

Dear Yvette: Happily Ever Now

Dear Yvette:

You never cease to amaze me.

Life's winds have blown, the storms have raged, but still you stand. To say you have been through a lot, would be an understatement.

Your journey has not been easy, but it has been necessary. Many of your lessons were difficult, but they were exactly what you needed to usher in your healing.

Love has been your greatest teacher – pushing you, pulling you, adding to, taking away, but all along, stretching and expanding you to experience it on a deeper and more compassionate level. No, not just that selective love that you show to complete strangers or that sister love you give to a new friend, but more the deep unconditional love – the very intimacy energy that created you. In-2-Me-I-See.

Unfortunately, the only way to bring forth that kind of love was to shatter the fairytale of what you thought love was, should be, and could be. Although it didn't look like the things you saw on TV or always felt like what your favorite love song described, amongst those scattered pieces, love was still very present and very real. Love has been your saving grace, ever-present as The Divine, who has always loved you.

You were loved so much, that you were given a mother and father who taught you that people can only do their best. They can only love at their greatest capacity.

You were loved so much, that you were instilled with the ability to have compassion for those who robbed you of your innocence, giving you the courage to love and care for others, at an early age.

You were loved so strongly, that you were blessed with the will to learn new ways of doing things. Even when you judged your trials as not good enough, love stepped in to connect you with better examples.

You were loved so much, that love allowed you to abort it before it would allow you to become overburdened with responsibilities you weren't fully capable of comprehending then. Love never gave up on you, it waited tirelessly and endlessly for the perfect moment to bless you twice over with smaller reflections of yourself. Reflections that you would learn to love so unconditionally that they would open the door for you to give and receive love on a bigger scale. An ideal mate for love.

You were loved so much, you were blessed with the gift to teach the very lessons that you were courageous enough to learn. It didn't stop there, you were offered this entire world as your classroom. You were loved so consistently, that love has been reflected back to you over and over again.

Even when you couldn't see the image clearly or simply refused to embrace it, love stood there, whispering to you softly, patiently waiting for the opportunity to reveal itself again. Yvette, you were loved so deeply, that it matched you with the perfect partner and life mate, music - your bi-sensual lover, teacher, and friend who will forever be your muse, your motivation, your inspiration for generations; your medicine when love hurts, your amulet when you need super powers.

Yvette, you are loved so immensely, that you've learned to experience love in its highest form. You have embraced forgiveness. You let go of the guilt and resentment.

No longer do you hide behind the hurt and shame of your past. No more are you suffocated by the pain and anger. Through forgiveness, you can breathe again, fresh new clean air. Inhale, exhale. Breathe new life into your very existence, into your experience. It is time to love in the present moment. For in this moment lies the love you have searched for, the love you've dreamed of, the love that has been there all along.

The love that is you.

Little did you know that sex would become your passport to healing. That using sex to find the love that you yearned for from your father would eventually lead you to a love that you had no idea existed within your SELF. A Love that is divinely connected to the Love that you share with the almighty Father.

This is what it feels like to be love and to be loved. It feels like accepting all of you. It feels like the gentle knowing that you are always loved. It feels like a kind reminder that because you are loved, you are also loveable. It feels like effortlessly allowing your loving reflections to show up, exactly as they are. It feels like a big kick in the face of happily ever after because you're in love with you happily ever now. Now you can move forward, in joy to experience the rest of your life with conscious love.

The best is yet to come. No- scratch that, the best kind of loving is here now because now you know true love.

I love you!

In gratitude & Love,
Yvette

Epilogue

Everyone wants the fairy tale, the perfect everything — life, mate, finances, career. How do you get to your perfected reality if you are chasing someone else's fantasy? How does perfect happen? If you have never seen it, how do you recognize it? Will you recognize it?

When you get on a rollercoaster, you know the dips and curves are coming and in anticipation you brace for the expected fall. When life throws a curve, there is no warning, and how you react—negatively or positively — will determine not only the outcome, but also your posture after the outcome. Will you make decisions based on past reactive tendencies? Or will you take possession and ownership of your life and make the decisions based on a different and desired outcome?

We are all equipped with a full arsenal to navigate this life. There is no situation or circumstance that we encounter that we have not been divinely given the answer. When we are continually faced with the same issue and predicament, and the knee jerk response is the same, be prepared, because the universe is a consistent and insistent teacher and will continue to place the same test on your desk until you get the answer right.

It takes a moment of selfish clarity to decide that you are deserving and valuable, and concentrated courage to take the steps to create your reality. When you become resolute about what you need for your perfected life, it will come and you will recognize it. Life is based on the laws of science and, fortunately, the rules are the same for us all - we attract what we reflect.

When we are moving in our true purpose and swimming in the pool that was divinely created for us, we do not have to pull, push or bend ourselves into intricate positions to fit into our own lives. We will never have to force anything or anyone into our world, because what belongs to us is already ours. What is divinely yours will flow through your life as effortlessly as water into a vase.

And now these three remain: faith, hope and love. But the greatest of these is love.

-I Corinthians 13:13

Thanks to science, there is a substitute for almost everything we eat, drink or wear. However what truly sustains us — faith, hope and love — have no equal, and a life well-lived cannot be complete without these three. —